SECRETS OF FAT-FREE KOSHER COOKING

Over 150 low-fat and fat-free traditional and contemporary recipes—from matzoh balls to kugel

DEBORAH BERNSTEIN, M.D.

Avery Publishing Group
Garden City Park, New York

D1312475

Cover Designer: William Gonzalez
Cover Photograph: Victor Giordano
Text Illustrator: John Wincek
Interior Color Photographs: Victor Giordano
Photo Food Stylist: BC Giordano
Typesetter: Elaine V. McCaw
In-House Editor: Marie Caratozzolo
Printer: Paragon Press, Honesdale, PA

Avery Publishing Group
120 Old Broadway
Garden City Park, NY 11040
1-800-548-5757

Cataloging-in-Publication Data

Bernstein, Deborah.
          Secrets of fat-free kosher cooking : over 170 low-fat and fat-free
    traditional and contemporary recipes—from matzoh balls to
    kugel / by Deborah Bernstein.
                  p.   cm.
          Includes index.
          ISBN 0-89529-806-6
             1. Low-fat diet—Recipes.   2. Cookery, Jewish.   I. Title.
    RM237.7.B455   1998
    641.5'638—dc21   97-28307
                                                                              CIP

Copyright © 1998 by Deborah Bernstein

Printed in the United States of America

10   9   8   7   6   5   4   3   2   1

Contents

To David
and
To my mother and father.

Acknowledgments

I would like to thank the following people, who were important in the creation of this book:

Managing editor Rudy Shur, editor Marie Caratozzolo, and everyone at Avery Publishing Group, for giving me the opportunity to publish this book and for the chance to work with such nice people.

My husband, David Kleinman, M.D., for patiently enduring endless variations of the recipes that led to this book.

My parents, Leo and Paula Bernstein, for their loving support and encouragement.

Rabbi Mordechai Willig of the Young Israel of Riverdale, Rosh Yeshiva of the Rabbi Isaac Elchanan Theological Seminary of Yeshiva University, for his clarification of the laws regarding kosher cooking and cooking for the Sabbath.

My friend, Jack Nuszen, D.O., who showed me that cooking for ten on a moment's notice can be fun.

And my best friend, Karen Cassouto Goliger, for listening to me kvetch.

Preface

COOKING 101

Learning to cook was a somewhat unusual experience for me. My wedding took place three days after my first year of medical school ended. I knew that for the next seven or eight years, I would be incredibly busy attending classes and serving my internship, residency, and fellowship. With these time constraints, I was afraid that I had to resign myself to meals that consisted of little more than canned tuna. I also knew that if I didn't learn to cook easy meals, inviting guests for dinner would probably occur only about once a year! This reality prompted me to learn to cook healthy kosher meals that were very, very quick and very, very easy.

Growing up, I learned a lot about cooking from my mother, who was my most invaluable resource for this cookbook. However, I also knew that I wouldn't be able to spend as much time preparing foods as she does. So I searched through cookbooks and other sources for recipes with kosher ingredients that were quick and easy to prepare, as well

as healthful. I found exactly none. Most cookbooks had recipes with about sixteen steps or more, along with a long list of hard-to-find ingredients. How was I going to find fresh chives, when I barely had the time to buy fresh milk? (Fat-free ice cream in your coffee does work, by the way.) Even recipes from a number of supposedly "easy" cookbooks often had instructions that read, "Begin to prepare this in the early afternoon." Obviously, these weren't going to work for my lifestyle.

I began to experiment with various recipes that I found in cookbooks and magazines. I modified ingredients to make each non-Kosher recipe kosher, and I tried eliminating needless steps to save time. It wasn't easy. I did find that many recipes had steps that were absolutely needless. For instance, I discovered that most ingredients do not have to be "pureed in small batches" or "strained three times through cheesecloth," and those recipes that require such steps are simply not for people with busy lives. Many times, however, my efforts had to be scrapped, and I found myself starting over again.

Shopping was another problem for me because of time constraints. I never knew when I would have time to shop, so I relied almost exclusively on nonperishable or frozen items. I bought a large spice rack and stocked it well with dried herbs and spices to always have on hand. I bought items like peanut butter, soy sauce, jellies and jams, pasta, and dried and canned beans. I bought a second freezer so I could stock up on frozen foods. It was important for me to be able to prepare quick-and-easy, yet healthful kosher meals, at least when I could stay awake long enough to eat them.

KOSHER AND OTHER ETHNIC DISHES

Kosher cooking has always had a reputation for being high in fat and calories; but, with a little creative work (elbow grease instead of schmaltz), most classic kosher dishes can be made fat-free or very-low fat without compromising the taste and texture of the originals. My fat-free hamantaschen, for example, gain their characteristic texture from fruit purée and egg whites, as do my fat-free kugels. And my Grandmother's split pea soup is made rich with the flavor of turkey pastrami instead of beef flanken.

I live in an urban multicultural neighborhood. To meet the needs of the residents, the local grocery stores carry a wide range of ethnic products, many of which have undergone kosher supervision. This has given me the wonderful opportunity to try new and different dishes and experiment with ingredients from the cuisines of many countries. French, Italian, Spanish, Chinese, Indian, and Mexican-style recipes, as well as dishes with a Caribbean island and American southwestern influence are presented in this book. All of these ethnic creations, which follow the laws of kosher cooking, are simple to prepare, fat-free or very low in fat, and absolutely delicious.

QUICK AND EASY COOKING

Quick and easy are two words that characterize my recipes, which have short preparation times—most can be prepared in under ten minutes, a few take less than two. They also require short cooking times and, best of all, an absolute minimum of fuss. Most recipes adhere to the following guideline: stir the ingredients together, cook them, and when the timer goes off, serve and enjoy.

Even during the most hectic years of my life, I found that I enjoyed cooking. For me it is a wonderfully creative outlet. My favorite challenge is to experiment with an ingredient to create a new dish, or bring an unusual twist to an old standby. My hope is that this cookbook will start you on your way to creating your own healthful and easy kosher dishes.

Introduction

While there are a number of kosher cookbooks on the market today, this is the first one that is geared exclusively toward delicious kosher dishes that are fat-free or very low in fat. During the early stages of this book, whenever I discussed its premise with my friends and colleagues, their reactions were always the same: "Tasty low-fat kosher? Impossible!" While I had to admit that kosher food does have the reputation for being high in fat, my health-conscious side as a physician made me determined to prove the skeptics wrong. I believed that with a few ingredient adjustments coupled with some sound cooking methods, I could create delicious low- and no-fat foods that are as high in nutrition as they are in flavor.

The result of my efforts proved fruitful. This book is bursting with delicious low-fat and fat-free traditional and contemporary kosher dishes, such as chicken soup with matzoh balls, gefilte fish, and a variety of kugels and chulents. There are also appetizers, entrées, side dishes, and desserts.

Yes, this book provides nutritious taste-tempting dishes that are amazingly quick and simple to prepare. But above all else, the recipes conform to the laws of *kashrus* (kosher foods), whose rich tradition is firmly rooted in the Bible. The following material highlights and summarizes the basic principles underlying this time-honored religious practice.

KOSHER CERTIFICATION

For a dish to be considered kosher, all of its ingredients must be certified through rabbinic supervision. There are several organizations in the United States and in countries throughout the world that perform this certification. Kosher foods and food products are easily identifiable by a symbol, which appears on their labels. This symbol usually represents the organization that has certified the product. For example, the letter "U" within a circle is the symbol of the Orthodox Union. Any label bearing this symbol signifies that the product has been certified kosher by the Orthodox Union—the largest kosher certification organization in the United States.

There are a number of national and regional organizations that perform this service, some of whose symbols are presented below.

Orthodox Union	*Star K*
Kof-K	*Organized Kashruth Laboratories*

Common Kosher Certification Symbols

While grocery shopping one day, I picked up a jar with a label that was written in Italian. I couldn't read the label, but I knew by the symbol that the product was certified kosher. Check with your local rabbinic authorities for appropriate certifications in your area.

Foods that are considered kosher are natural products, such as fruits, vegetables, legumes, and grains. These items must be checked for insects and thoroughly washed before eating. However, foods that have additives and/or are processed, require verification that all of the added ingredients are kosher. Some commonly used additives are not necessarily kosher. For example, gelatin, which is found in a number of products, and renin, which is used in cheese production, must come from kosher-certified animals. Lecithin must be derived from soybeans or eggs, and pectin must come from citrus fruits or apples.

The laws of kosher food also place restrictions on the way in which foods are processed.

Any equipment used for processing cannot also be used for non-kosher products, nor can it be used for processing both meat and dairy products.

For a meat to be kosher, it must come from a kosher animal (one that has split hooves and chews it cud). This includes cows, sheep, goats, and deer. Fowl that are considered kosher include chickens, turkeys, ducks, and geese. The animal must be ritually slaughtered in compliance with Jewish law, and then soaked and salted in a prescribed manner before being cooked. In the United States, reputable kosher butchers sell meat and poultry that has been slaughtered appropriately and then soaked and salted. The consumer has only to buy the meat or poultry, bring it home, and cook it. The exception is liver. Liver does not need to be soaked and salted, but it must be broiled before it is eaten. Meat that is certified *glatt kosher* signifies that the lungs of the animal were "glatt" or smooth and free of lesions. The glatt kosher certification indicates a stricter level of kosher supervision.

Many supermarkets throughout the United States sell frozen kosher meats and poultry. Often these products are stocked in a special freezer area, apart from the non-kosher foods. Already soaked and salted these kosher meats and poultry are ready to be cooked.

Like meats and poultry, milk and other dairy products need proper rabbinic supervision to certify that they are kosher. The milk must come from a kosher animal and must not be mixed with meat. And the equipment used for processing cannot also be used for meat products or non-kosher products.

Fish that have fins and scales, such as pike, carp, cod, bass, perch, flounder, tuna, salmon, red snapper, and sable, are considered kosher. Shellfish are not. There are comprehensive lists of kosher fish available from rabbinic authorities.

In most parts of the United States, kosher products are readily available in local supermarkets. Recently, a growing number of manufacturers have begun requesting kosher certification of their products. This has resulted in the appearance of new kosher items on store shelves, giving the kosher cook an incredible opportunity to experiment with foods that were previously unavailable. I have been having a lot of fun trying out some of these new products, which include a variety of fat-free cheeses and dairy products, baked goods, condiments, salsas, and sauces.

COOKING AND EATING KOSHER

The laws of kosher cooking do not allow the mixing of meat (*fleishig*) and milk (*milchig*) products in the same dish, nor are they allowed to be eaten at the same meal. This separation of meat and dairy stems from the passage, "Seethe not the kid in its mother's milk," which is mentioned three times in the Bible.

Two sets of dishes, pots, and utensils are needed in a kosher kitchen—one set for meats, the other for milk and other dairy products. These items should also be stored separately. It is important to have a simple system that makes it easy to recognize which set of utensils and equipment are for meat and which are for dairy. Some people buy two sets of utensils in different colors to distinguish them from each other, while others paint a small patch of color on one of the sets. And some people simply designate separate cabinets for the sets. I have one set of blue dishes for meat and another set of peach dishes for dairy. I cook meats in one brand of pots and pans and dairy in another. And the pattern on my meat silverware is different from my dairy utensils. You may find another system that works best for you. The important thing is to organize your kitchen equipment so it is easy to identify.

After eating a meat meal, it is customary to wait six hours before eating a dairy meal. After consuming a dairy meal, a period of one hour must elapse and the mouth should be rinsed before eating meat.

Foods that are neither meat nor dairy, such as vegetables, eggs, fish, coffee, tea, salt, and sugar, are considered *pareve* and may be eaten with either meat or dairy foods. Fish, although a pareve food, should not be eaten together with meat or fowl. It may, however, be eaten either before or after these foods, on a separate dish and with another fork.

Many people keep a few pots and utensils just for pareve foods. If a pareve food is to be eaten only with other pareve foods, it may be prepared with pareve, meat, or dairy pots and utensils. If a pareve food is to be eaten with meat, it may be cooked with either pareve or meat pots and utensils. If a pareve food is to be eaten with dairy, it may be prepared with either pareve or dairy pots and utensils.

COOKING FOR THE SABBATH

The Jewish Sabbath begins eighteen minutes before sundown on Friday and ends one hour and ten minutes past sunset on Saturday. All forms of cooking are prohibited on the Sabbath. Foods that are to be eaten warm during this time should be at least halfway cooked before the Sabbath begins. The food is then kept warm in a crockpot or slow-cooker. Cooked food can also be put in a pot and placed over a lit burner on a large metal sheet called a *blech*. (For more information on crockpots, slow-cookers, and blechs, *see* pages 67 and 68.) Soups and stews are traditionally eaten during the Sabbath.

USING THE RECIPES IN THIS COOKBOOK

When purchasing ingredients to create the

dishes in this book, be sure to check product labels for kosher certification. Buy meats and poultry from a reputable kosher butcher. When buying meats and poultry from your local supermarket, buy only those products that bear symbols certifying that they are kosher.

Recipes in this cookbook that include meat are meant to be eaten only with other meat or pareve foods. Recipes with dairy ingredients are meant to be eaten only with other dairy or pareve foods. And those recipes with ingredients that are pareve may be eaten with either meat or dairy foods. And, as mentioned earlier, fish, like other pareve foods, may be eaten together with dairy foods. However, fish and meat, although permitted to be eaten at the same meal, should be eaten as separate courses using different utensils.

All of the recipes in this book conform to the laws of kosher cooking. The ingredients are easy to find, and the dishes are quick and easy to prepare, healthful, and, best of all, delicious. Remember, you don't have to be Jewish to enjoy the *Secrets of Fat-Free Kosher Cooking*.

1.
Fat-Free Cooking

As a physician, I am very aware of the importance of eating healthful foods and lowering dietary fat. Not only does a low-fat diet help people lose weight, it also helps decrease the risk of many diseases associated with obesity, such as high blood pressure, diabetes, atherosclerotic heart disease, and many forms of cancer.

Keep in mind, however, that low-fat does not necessarily mean low-calorie. Do you know that although many commercially prepared foods may be fat-free, high levels of sugar and sodium have been added for enhanced flavor? This results in low-fat and fat-free foods that are very high in calories and low in nutritional value.

Although the recipes in this book contain little or no fat, their flavor comes from only nutritious, low-calorie ingredients. My goal was to create a wide variety of quick and easy fat-free and low-fat kosher dishes that are both healthful and delicious.

This chapter will explain the importance of reducing dietary fat, while teaching you how to budget your daily fat and caloric intake. It also details the best ingredients to use in your delicious, nutritious no-fat and low-fat kosher creations.

THE PROBLEM WITH FAT

Fat itself is not bad; it is essential to the body's functioning. The problem comes from too much fat in our diets.

Fat is a combination of hydrogen, oxygen, and carbon, as are all carbohydrates. However, it is has twice as many calories as carbohydrates and protein. To illustrate this point, compare a cup of corn oil (pure fat) with a cup of flour (almost pure carbohydrates). The oil has over 1,900 calories, while the flour has only 400. When one gram of fat is burned by the body for fuel, it produces 9 calories of energy, but when one gram of carbohydrate or protein is burned for fuel, it produces only 4 calories worth of energy. It is also easier for the body to store fat as fat than it is to store carbohydrates or proteins as fat.

When eaten in excess, fat is readily converted into body fat. When foods that are high in carbohydrates are eaten in excess, they are also stored as fat, but they must first go through a conversion process, which burns up some of the carbohydrates. So even though a high-fat diet and a high-carbohydrate diet may contain the same number of calories, the high-fat diet will result in about 20 percent more in weight gain than the carbohydrate diet.

Not only does the consumption of too much fat lead to excessive weight gain, it puts one at a greater risk for heart disease, diabetes, and certain cancers, including cancer of the breast, uterus, and colon. There are three major types of fat—saturated, polyunsaturated, and monounsaturated.

Saturated fat is found primarily in animal products, including dairy items, such as whole milk, cream, and cheese, and fatty meats like beef, veal, and lamb. Some vegetable products, including coconut oil, palm kernel oil, and vegetable shortening, are also high in saturated fat. Excessive dietary intake of saturated fats can significantly elevate blood cholesterol levels, increasing the risk of heart disease.

Polyunsaturated fat is found in corn, sunflower, and safflower oils, and products made from these oils. Although polyunsaturates may actually lower cholesterol levels, in doing so, they also tend to reduce high density lipoproteins (HDLs)—your "good" cholesterol. Excessive amounts of polyunsaturated fat are also suspect in high blood pressure and blood clot development.

Monounsaturated fat is abundant in certain nuts, such as peanuts, cashews, and almonds, and some vegetable and nut oils, such as olive, peanut, and canola. Some studies have shown that monounsaturates, used in small amounts, may actually help decrease the risk of heart disease. The people of Mediterranean regions, whose diets typically include olive oil, have low rates of cardiovascular disease.

Trans-fatty acids are fats that have been chemically altered through hydrogenation. This process, which adds hydrogen to vegetable oils, transforms them into solid shortenings and margarines. Hydrogenation extends the oil's shelf life and improves its qualities in baking and cooking; however, the trans-fatty acids it creates cause similar negative side effects as saturated fats.

THE GOOD NEWS ABOUT FAT

One might conclude that fat, with all of its negative side effects, should be banned completely from our diets. Do we need fat at all? The answer is a resounding "yes." Some dietary fat is essential in maintaining cell walls, in storing and circulating fat-soluble vitamins (A, D, E, and K), and in performing other functions to sustain a healthy body.

Linoleic acid, a polyunsaturated fat found in oils such as corn, soy, and safflower, as well as walnuts, pine nuts, and sesame and sunflower seeds, is necessary for good health. The average adult requires a daily minimum of 3 to 6 grams of linoleic acid (approximately two teaspoons of polyunsaturated vegetable oil or two tablespoons of nuts or seeds). Another essential fat—linolenic acid—is also essential for good health. It is found mainly in fish and green plants.

Yes, fat is essential for life. The problem occurs when people consume too much.

DAILY FAT YOU CAN LIVE WITH

The average American consumes 40 percent of his or her calories from fat in a typical day. The American Dietetic Association and the American Heart Association suggest that no more than 30 percent of one's daily calories come from fat, and 20 to 25 percent would be even better. No more than 10 percent of these calories should come from saturated fats.

With the amount of daily fat you eat based on caloric intake, you must first establish how many calories you need in a day. Individual calorie needs differ depending on a person's weight, age, sex, rate of metabolism, and activity level. Generally, however, in order for most adults to maintain their weight, they must consume about 15 calories for each pound they weigh.

To establish your personal maximum daily calorie and fat intake, follow the steps presented here:

1. First, determine the number of calories your body needs in one day. This number depends on your body weight. Let's say, for instance, you weigh 130 pounds. To maintain this body weight, you would need to consume approximately 15 calories for every pound you weigh—about 1,950 calories:

$$\begin{array}{rl} 130 & \text{pounds (total body weight)} \\ \underline{\times\ 15} & \text{calories (per pound)} \\ 1,950 & \text{total daily calories (needed} \\ & \text{to maintain body weight)} \end{array}$$

2. Multiply the total daily calories by 0.25 (25 percent) to determine the maximum number of daily calories that should come from fat:

$$\begin{array}{rl} 1,950 & \text{total daily calories} \\ \underline{\times\ 0.25} & \text{percent} \\ 487 & \text{total calories from fat} \end{array}$$

3. As 1 gram of fat has 9 calories, divide the total daily calories by 9 to determine the total fat-gram allowance:

$$\begin{array}{rl} 487 & \text{total calories from fat} \\ \underline{\div\ 9} & \text{calories per fat gram} \\ 54 & \text{total daily fat grams} \end{array}$$

4. As no more than 10 percent of one's daily fat calories should come from saturated fat, simply divide the total daily calories by 10 percent, then divide by 9:

$$\begin{array}{rl} 1,950 & \text{total daily calories} \\ \underline{\div\ .10} & \text{percent} \\ 195 & \text{total saturated fat calories} \\ \underline{\div\ \ \ 9} & \text{calories per fat gram} \\ 21 & \text{total saturated fat grams} \end{array}$$

To summarize, a typical, moderately active 130-pound person should consume approximately 1,950 daily calories. No more than 487 of these calories should come from fat (54 grams) with less than 195 fat calories (21 grams) coming from saturated fat.

The handy table presented below shows the suggested maximum daily calories for a variety of different weights, along with a fat-gram budget based on 25 percent of these daily calories. If you are overweight, choose your goal weight, and follow the appropriate allowances. Keep in mind that these figures are approximate.

Daily Fat Intake Chart

Weight in pounds	Recommended Daily Calories (15 calories per pound)	Total Fat Grams (25% of total daily calories)	Total Saturated Fat Grams (10% of total fat calories)
100	1,500	42	16
110	1,650	46	18
120	1,800	50	20
130	1,950	54	22
140	2,100	58	23
150	2,250	62	25
160	2,400	67	27
170	2,550	71	28
180	2,700	75	30
190	2,850	79	32
200	3,000	83	33

BEWARE: LOW-FAT IS NOT NECESSARILY LOW-CALORIE

Americans are becoming more and more weight conscious. Since the 1980s, they have reduced their consumption of fat considerably. Why then has the rate of obesity increased in this country? The answer is obvious. While people may be keeping an eye on their fat intake, they are consuming more calories, and they are not exercising enough. Many people do not realize that those excess calories count.

With all of the fat-free and reduced-fat products bombarding grocery store shelves, people are mistakenly consuming mass quantities of these foods with little thought to the number of calories they include. Many of these products have high levels of sugar and other high-calorie flavor enhancers. And any food eaten in excess of calories burned in a day will be converted to body fat.

If you stay within your fat budget and choose to eat foods that are nutritious, you will likely have no trouble reaching or maintaining your goal weight

WHAT ABOUT CHOLESTEROL?

Cholesterol is a fatty substance found in all foods that come from animal sources, such as meats, eggs, poultry, fish, and dairy products. Our bodies need cholesterol, which helps to build cell membranes and nerve cell sheaths. Cholesterol also helps produce hormones, bile acids (necessary to aid digestion), and vitamin D. The liver is capable of producing all of the cholesterol needed for good health.

Cholesterol is carried through the blood by lipoproteins. High density lipoproteins (HDLs)—considered the "good" cholesterol—carry cholesterol throughout the body and return it to the liver for processing. The other type of lipoprotein—low-density lipoproteins (LDLs)—can allow cholesterol to be "dropped off" and remain as deposits in blood vessels. These deposits build up in arteries and can lead to high blood pressure, stroke, and heart disease. HDLs can sometimes remove the cholesterol deposits left by the LDLs.

The average American consumes too much cholesterol—between 450 and 500 milligrams per day. The United States Food and Drug Administration (FDA) and the Department of Agriculture (USDA) recommend a maximum of 300 milligrams of cholesterol per day. This is also the recommendation of the American Heart Association, the National Academy of Sciences, and the National Institutes of Health. These organizations further recommend that people with severe high blood cholesterol or heart disease limit their cholesterol intake even further.

Studies have indicated that diets that include oat bran, barley, and fish oils appear to lower cholesterol levels in the blood. However, the most reliable way to lower one's cholesterol level is by reducing the amount of dietary cholesterol. In some instances, medication from a physician may be necessary to help lower these levels.

IMPORTANCE OF FIBER

Dietary fiber, a complex carbohydrate, is found in plants—in the outer layers of cereal grains, and the fibrous parts of fruits, beans, and other vegetables. Fiber is actually the part of the plant that our body cannot digest.

Fiber performs a number of important functions that help a body maintain optimal health. It promotes feelings of fullness; prevents constipation, hemorrhoids, and other intestinal problems; and is associated with reduced incidence of colon cancer. In addition, fiber may help lower blood cholesterol levels, reducing the risk of heart disease.

The recommended amount of daily fiber is 11.5 grams per 1,000 calories—approximately 20 to 30 grams for the average adult. Most American adults, however, consume only about 4 to 6 grams of fiber each day.

MAINTAINING A HEALTHFUL DIET

In 1992, the United States Department of Agriculture presented the Food Guide Pyramid (*see* figure below). This graphic is the primary device for educating the public about its daily nutritional needs.

Bread, cereal, rice, and pasta form the broad base of the pyramid; 6 to 11 servings of these foods are suggested daily. The narrower second pyramid level includes fruits (2 to 4 servings) and vegetables (3 to 5 servings). The next level includes dairy products (2 to 3 servings) and a group that includes meat, poultry, fish, dry beans, eggs, and nuts (2 to 3 servings). The pyramid's small triangular top level includes fats, oils, and sweets, which are to be eaten sparingly.

Choosing the Best Ingredients and Cooking Methods

Preparing fat-free and low-fat kosher dishes has become increasingly easy because of the many reduced-fat products that are readily available on grocery store shelves. You can also purchase kosher food products via mail order. To receive a copy of *To Life—the Healthy Kosher Gourmet Catalog*, call 1 (800) 317–3449.

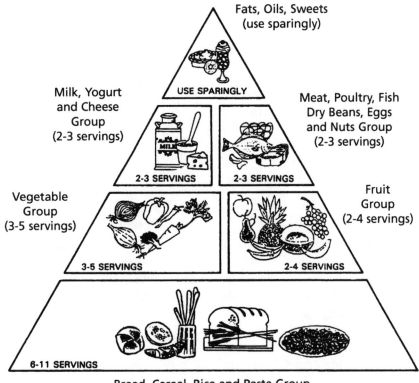

The Food Guide Pyramid

MEATS, POULTRY, AND VEGETARIAN ALTERNATIVES

Whether you are a confirmed meat eater, someone who eats meat occasionally, or a vegetarian, know that plenty of lean meats and poultry, as well as excellent meat substitutes, are readily available.

Beef

Due to the high fat and cholesterol content of beef, its use in a healthful diet should be limited. More and more consumers are demanding leaner cuts of beef from their butchers and grocers. The good news is many beef producers have changed the breeding and feeding habits of their cattle. The result is meats that are considerably leaner than they were in the past. And butchers are trimming more of the fat from retail cuts of beef before selling it to their customers.

Be aware, however, that even lean cuts of beef have varying amounts of fat due to their grade differences. The more expensive USDA Prime and Choice grades of meat generally contain more fat that the other grades. This fat is marbleized within the beef and cannot be trimmed away. Beef with the least amount of marbleized fat is USDA Select. Veal, which is lean and low in fat, is a good alternative to beef.

Chicken

Chicken is lower in fat content and calories than most cuts of beef and veal. The white meat of a chicken is lower in fat than the dark meat. The skin should always be removed. Some cuts of chicken, if eaten with the skin, contain more fat than some cuts of beef.

A 3.5-ounce serving of skinless white meat chicken contains 173 calories and 4.5 grams of fat. The same size serving of skinless dark meat chicken has 205 calories and 9.7 grams of fat. Most of the chicken recipes in this

book call for skinless, boneless white meat chicken breasts. Not only are skinless chicken breasts lower in fat than other chicken parts, they require the shortest cooking time.

Always keep uncooked chicken refrigerated to prevent bacterial growth, and defrost frozen chicken in the refrigerator, not on the kitchen counter. Wash the chicken well before cooking it. Be sure to wash all surfaces and utensils that have come in contact with raw chicken with soap and hot water.

Turkey

Skinless white meat turkey is even lower in fat content than skinless white meat chicken. Compared to a 3.5-ounce serving of chicken (173 calories and 4.5 grams of fat), the same amount of skinless white meat turkey has only 157 calories and 3.2 grams of fat.

While turkey is a great choice for healthy meals, many people find it dry and tough. When prepared properly, however, its texture is similar to chicken. I find that cooking turkey slowly at a low temperature is one way to keep it moist. Covering a turkey roast with juice- or soup-moistened slices of bread is another trick to keep it from drying out as it cooks. When you try the turkey recipes in this cookbook, you will be surprised to find that turkey can be moist, juicy, and flavorful.

Like chicken, uncooked turkey should be kept refrigerated to prevent bacterial growth. Any countertops and utensils that have come into contact with raw turkey must be washed thoroughly with soap and hot water.

Ground Meats

It's no surprise that of all the ground meat varieties, skinless white meat turkey contains the least amount of fat—only 1 percent by weight. Even skinless dark meat turkey is only 8 to 10 percent fat by weight. Beware of brands that include skin and added fat. They can contain as much as 15 percent fat. Like ground turkey, ground chicken can also be very low in fat provided skinless white meat is used. Ground veal, while slightly higher in fat than chicken or turkey, contains less fat than regular ground beef. While ground beef is higher in fat and calories than the other meats, low-fat ground beef is also available. The leanest ground beef sold today is 95 percent lean.

I use ground turkey in any recipe that calls for ground meat. Unfortunately, ground turkey has a reputation for being rather dry and lacking flavor. I have found, however, that the right blending of herbs, spices, and other flavorful ingredients, coupled with proper cooking methods can result in delicious ground turkey dishes.

If your family really doesn't want ground turkey, try ground skinless white-meat chicken, which is also very low in fat. But if it's ground meat and not ground poultry that your family is clamoring for, try mixing ground turkey with ground veal. This flavorful mixture does have a bit more fat than ground turkey alone, but not a substantial amount. You can also try mixing the leanest ground beef you can find with ground veal, turkey, and/or chicken. This will lower the fat content while preserving the flavor of the beef. Gradually try to increase the amount of veal, turkey, or chicken in the mixture until your family gets used to the taste. Before you know it, you will have stopped using beef altogether.

Vegetarian Meat Alternatives

For those of you who prefer a nonmeat alternative to ground meat, there are a number of options. I prefer using vegetable protein crumbles. With a texture similar to ground meat, vegetable protein crumbles, a pareve food, are a healthy fat-free meat substitute. Green Giant makes a vegetable protein product that is readily available in many supermarkets. Texturized vegetable protein (TVP), which is made from defatted soy flour, is another good alternative to ground meat.

FISH

Some fish are moderately fatty, while others, such as halibut, cod, and sole, are practically fat-free. Omega-3 fatty acids, the oils found in fish, may be helpful in lowering cholesterol and blood pressure, and preventing the formation of blood clots. Studies have shown that groups of people who eat large amounts of fish, such as the Japanese and the Eskimos, have the lowest rates of heart disease in the world. In other words, even the fatty varieties of fish are considered healthful.

When shopping for fish, be sure to choose the freshest available. For whole fish, choose ones with shiny skin and bright red gills that spread easily when opened. Fish fillets should have firm flesh. Fresh fish has a clean fresh scent, not a "fishy" odor. Because it is highly perishable, fish should be refrigerated and cooked the same day or shortly after it is purchased. Frozen fish lack the texture and taste of fresh, but may be substituted for fresh fish in any recipe.

In order for a fish to be considered kosher, it must have fins and scales. Shellfish are not kosher. If you have any question regarding which fish are kosher, check with your local rabbi. He can direct you to a comprehensive list of kosher varieties. The fish called for in this book include flounder, cod, perch (whiting), tuna, red snapper, salmon, and pollock. Unless otherwise specified, fillets are skinless and boneless; whole fish have been cleaned (gutted) and scaled.

Fish heads and bones can be used to make flavorful stock to use in fish soups and stews.

Bones from any type of kosher fish and in any combination may be used. Fish stores are usually quite happy to give away these fish parts. Just make sure the gills and eyes have been removed. The recipe for a rich, flavorful fish stock is found on page 40.

BEANS, GRAINS, AND SOY PRODUCTS

Considered kosher, whole grains and whole grain products are nutritionally rich. In addition to containing valuable nutrients such as vitamin E, zinc, potassium, magnesium, and chromium, they also contain fiber, which is important in a healthy diet. Fiber promotes a feeling of fullness, which makes meals more satisfying.

The following products are used in the recipes throughout this book. Many are readily available in most supermarkets, while others are stock items in health food stores.

Barley

Considered one of the oldest cultivated grains, barley has a nutty flavor and unique texture that makes it a wonderful addition to soups, stews, and casseroles. It is also a great substitute for rice in many dishes. Even after cooking in a crockpot for hours, barley still retains its flavor and shape.

Beans

Beans, or more accurately, legumes, are the fruit of leguminous plants. These plants form hanging pods and within these pods are found the peas, lentils, and bean varieties that have fed man for centuries. Fresh, garden variety green beans and peas are "immature" legumes. When these seeds are allowed to mature and dry on the plant, their nutritional value increases significantly. High in fiber with virtually no fat, dried legumes are rich in protein, iron, calcium, and B vitamins.

With the exception of split peas and lentils, dried beans benefit from presoaking before they are cooked (*see* instructions on page 29). Most dried beans are perfect to use in crockpot-cooked stews. In most recipes, feel free to substitute dried beans with cooked canned varieties.

Brown Rice

This tender, moist rice has a nutty flavor and slightly chewy texture. Because it retains its bran coat and germ, it is considered a whole-kernel rice. Brown rice is rich in protein, fiber, vitamin E, iron, calcium, phosphorus, and most of the B vitamins. Since its kernel has not been removed, brown rice has more nutrients and fiber than white rice.

Oat Bran

The outer part of the oat kernel, oat bran is a great source of fiber. It helps retain moisture in baked goods, so it is perfect for baking. Oat bran is also believed to lower blood cholesterol levels.

Tofu

Made from soybeans, tofu—also known as bean curd—is touted by many as the perfect food. It is low in fat, high in protein and calcium, and contains no cholesterol. In addition, tofu contains all eight essential amino acids. Having very little taste, tofu absorbs the flavors of its surrounding ingredients. Tofu with kosher certification is available in supermarkets and can also be ordered through the mail.

Whole Wheat Flour

The ground germ and bran of the whole

wheat berry, whole wheat flour is nutritionally superior to refined flour. While whole wheat flour works well for muffins and loaf cakes, it may be too heavy in some cakes and pastries.

Wild Rice

Wild rice has a sweet nutty flavor and is particularly high in protein and fiber. A great choice for crockpots, wild rice retains its shape and flavor even after many hours of cooking.

DAIRY PRODUCTS

There are fat-free and low-fat versions of most dairy products. Use the following items when preparing the recipes in this book.

Milk

With 0.5 grams of fat per cup, skim milk is obviously the better low-fat choice than whole milk, which contains 8 grams of fat per cup. Another good choice is 1-percent milk, which contains 2 grams of fat per cup. In my recipes, skim milk is always used. When using non-dairy creamers, such as Coffee Rich, for pareve recipes, always choose the reduced-fat or fat-free version.

Cheese

Low-fat and fat-free cheeses, including mozzarella, American, Muenster, cheddar, and Parmesan, are becoming increasingly popular. Cream cheese, cottage, and farmer cheese are also available in fat-free and reduced-fat versions. If you are used to full-fat cheeses, it might be best to first switch to a low-fat (part skim) variety before attempting the transition to fat-free. Also, be sure to try different brands, as there is a lot of variation in the quality of these dairy products.

Nondairy cheese alternatives are great for recipes with meat or for those who are lactose intolerant. Be aware that brands differ enormously in both taste and texture. Try different brands until you find one or two best suited for your recipes. And always check the labels carefully as some cheese substitutes may, in fact, be dairy.

SALAD DRESSINGS AND SPREADS

Flavorful, rich spreads and salad dressings have always had the reputation for being high in both fat and calories. Thankfully, like most dairy products, reduced-fat and fat-free dressings are available today.

Regular mayonnaise is nearly 100 percent fat. Fat-free mayonnaise, as well as reduced-fat varieties that contain up to two-thirds less fat than the regular, are healthy alternatives. Good choices include Weight Watchers, Hellman's, Smart Beat, and Miracle Whip. As some fat-free spreads are dairy, be sure to check labels carefully. Some fat-free spreads, both full and reduced-fat, may be pareve. And when looking to substitute mayonnaise in a dairy recipe, try fat-free yogurt.

Fat-free salad dressings also come in a wide variety of delicious flavors. Use these dressings, instead of their fat-filled counterparts, to dress up salads, flavor vegetables, and add zing to grilled foods. Again, check labels carefully as some fat-free salad dressings are dairy.

EGGS AND EGG WHITES

Those who cook know the importance of eggs, especially in baked goods. However, as valuable as eggs are, they also contain fat and high levels of cholesterol. Compare one large egg, which contains 5 grams of fat and 210 milligrams of cholesterol, to the equivalent amount of egg white or fat-free egg substitute, which contains no fat and no cholesterol. With the exception of Guilt-Free Matzoh Balls (page 45) and Grandma Helen's Hamantaschen (page 204), all of the recipes in this cookbook use egg whites instead of whole eggs—2 large egg whites are equivalent to 1 large egg. You can also use fat-free egg substitute—3 table-spoons of egg substitute are equivalent to 1 large egg—if you prefer. The egg whites called for in my recipes are from medium-sized eggs.

FAT SUBSTITUTES FOR BAKING

In baking, a number of fat-free ingredients make excellent substitutes for the usual oil, butter, and margarine. Fruit purées, as well as unsweetened applesauce, add texture and moistness to baked goods. Unsweetened applesauce, which comes in convenient 4-ounce containers and may be stored unrefrigerated before opening, can be purchased plain or with added fruits such as cranberries and raspberries. Unsweetened pear baby food adds a light flavor to baked goods, while unsweetened prune butter (lekvar) is a wonderful addition to chocolate baked goods. Unsweetened apple butter, pumpkin purée, and puréed zucchini are all good fat substitutes in muffins and cakes.

SWEETENERS

Although in some recipes granulated white sugar is necessary for texture and taste, I try to use it sparingly as it is high in calories and lacks nutritional value. Whenever possible, I prefer to use fruit juices, fruit purées, molasses, honey, and spices such as cinnamon and nutmeg to add sweetness to my recipes. I also use brown sugar, which, although high in calories, contains more calcium, iron, and potassium than refined white sugar. And because brown sugar is sweeter than white sugar, less is needed.

Apple juice concentrate, and pineapple, orange, and white grape juice are wonderful, low-calorie sweeteners for muffins, cakes, and kugel. I always keep some frozen varieties on hand. Honey adds both sweetness and moistness to baked goods, while fruit purées are valuable as sweeteners as well as fat substitutes.

OILS AND COOKING SPRAYS

Even when you are cooking "low-fat," a little bit of oil is sometimes necessary to enhance flavor, prevent sticking, or promote the browning of food. Because monounsaturated fats—typically olive and canola oil—appear to be linked to a lower risk of heart disease, these are the only oils I call for in my recipes. And then, only in very small amounts.

Nonstick vegetable-oil cooking sprays are very useful when preparing low-fat and reduced-fat meals. Although cooking sprays are 100 percent fat, the amount that comes out in a spray is so small that the added fat is insignificant. These sprays come in unflavored varieties, as well as butter and olive oil flavors. Recently, flavorful Oriental, garlic, Italian, and mesquite sprays have made their way to store shelves.

SALT

Salt has long been a flavor enhancer for many foods. This combination of sodium and chloride, however, has been implicated in a number of dangerous conditions, including high blood pressure. The American Heart Association considers 3,000 milligrams of sodium—about 1 teaspoon of salt—the daily maximum for the average person. Those with high blood pressure should further restrict dietary salt.

The recipes in this cookbook have no added salt. The wise use of flavorful herbs and spices eliminates the need for salt without compromising taste.

HERBS AND SPICES

Enhancing both the flavor and aroma of foods, herbs and spices are especially important in healthful fat-free cooking. They allow for the elimination of fat and salt without compromising taste. There are many traditional uses of herbs and spices—oregano is characteristically used in Italian tomato sauces, paprika is typical in Hungarian goulash, cardamom is common to Indian dishes—but don't feel limited to such standard uses. Many of the kosher recipes in this book utilize common spices and herbs from many different cuisines, resulting in new and appealing flavor combinations.

Allspice. Made from the ground berry of the West Indian myrtle tree, allspice tastes like a blend of cloves, cinnamon, and nutmeg.

Basil. The distinctly pungent basil leaf enhances robust foods such as beans, pastas, and stews. It goes exceptionally well with tomatoes and other vegetables. Basil grows well in a windowsill pot or herb garden.

Bay leaf. The aromatic bay leaf is frequently used to add richness to meat and poultry dishes, as well as soups, stews, and sauces. Be sure to remove this inedible leaf from the dish before serving.

Cardamom. Native to India, cardamom is a member of the ginger family. The sweet, strong-flavored seeds, which come encased in pods, are generally removed and crushed before using. Cardamom pods may be used whole to impart both flavor and aroma. Remove before serving to lessen the spiciness of the dish.

Cinnamon. Commonly used to flavor fruits and a variety of baked goods, cinnamon comes from the dried inner bark of the small tropical laurel tree.

Clove. The dried flower buds of a tropical evergreen tree, cloves are used to flavor soups, broths, and stews. Ground clove is sometimes used to spice up fruit dishes. Cloves are traditionally used in the ritual of Havdalah after the Sabbath.

Coriander seeds. Dried coriander seeds have a sweet taste that is reminiscent of lemon peel and sage. It is commonly used as a pickling spice and as an ingredient in curried dishes.

Crushed red pepper. Made from the seeds and skin of the red chili pepper, flavorful crushed red pepper is sold as dried flakes. Just a small amount releases a substantial amount of heat, so use it with discretion.

Cumin. Ground or whole cumin has a warm, nutty aroma and taste. It is popularly used in Mexican, Spanish, Indian, and Middle Eastern-style dishes. Cumin adds a deep hearty flavor to chilies and stews.

Curry powder. Curry powder is the blended mixture of a number of spices including cardamom, cayenne, cloves, coriander, cumin, dill weed, ginger, mace, pepper, and turmeric. It is popularly used in Indian-style dishes.

Dill weed. The leaves of the dill plant, aromatic dill weed has a subtle licorice taste. It is commonly used to flavor soups, sauces, and dips. Dill weed grows beautifully in a windowsill pot or herb garden.

Garlic. This pungent herb is an essential ingredient used to flavor a wide variety of dishes. Its peeled cloves are usually minced or crushed to release their distinctive flavor. Although fresh garlic is readily available year round, convenient jars of minced or chopped garlic are also found on grocery store shelves.

Ginger. Thinly sliced or peeled fresh ginger adds unique flavor to stews, sauces, and Oriental dishes. Ground ginger finds use in a variety of baked goods.

Mace. Made from nutmeg's lacy red outer

covering, mace is commonly used to flavor muffins and other spiced baked goods.

Marjoram. Strong, sweet, sage-like flavored marjoram is used to season meats and flavor a variety of vegetables and legumes.

Mint. Fresh mint is a flavorful addition for many fruit desserts, beverages, and a variety of vegetable and grain dishes. You can grow mint at home with minimum care.

Nutmeg. Made from the dried seeds of the tropical nutmeg tree, ground nutmeg is popularly used in a number of baked goods. It is also used in discreet amounts in some savory dishes.

Oregano. This powerful herb is frequently used in Italian cooking to flavor tomato sauces, soups, and stews. Dried oregano is more potent than fresh.

Paprika. This spice comes from the dried ripe pods of the largest and mildest varieties of the capsicum shrubs (pepper plants). Different varieties of paprika vary in pungency, with the best coming from Hungary. It is used to add both color and flavor to dishes.

Parsley. Flat-leafed parsley adds mild flavor to foods without overpowering them. When purchasing fresh parsley, choose the flat-leafed variety over the curly leafed, which is less flavorful. Parsley grows easily in a windowsill pot or herb garden.

Rosemary. Resembling short, thick pine needles, rosemary has a characteristic fresh, woodsy flavor that goes well with many poultry dishes and stews.

Sage. This herb has a pale green fuzzy leaf and a strong distinctive flavor that complements stuffings, soups, and stews.

Savory. Adding a pleasant, piquant flavor to vegetables and all types of bean dishes, savory is also a wonderful addition to stews.

Tarragon. Delicate-flavored tarragon is an important herb in French cooking. It is used to flavor meats, fish, and poultry, and is a delicious addition to salads and sauces.

Thyme. A strong herb with a warm, pungent flavor, thyme enhances the taste of many foods, including dried beans, stews, and a variety of vegetables.

Turmeric. Made from the dried root of a plant in the ginger family, turmeric has a bitter, somewhat gingery taste. It imparts a warm, appealing yellow color and an appetizing aroma to soups and stews.

COOKING EQUIPMENT

Do you need special equipment for fat-free cooking? Not really. You need only a few simple items to prepare your delicious meals.

Nonstick Pots and Skillets

Oil prevents food from sticking to a pot or skillet and burning. With a nonstick pot or skillet, you can use a minimum amount of oil—often just a light coating of cooking spray—when preparing foods. As an added bonus, nonstick cookware is a snap to clean.

Crockpots and Slow-Cookers

A crockpot is an electric cooker that maintains a low temperature. A slow-cooker is a baking dish that rests on a tray with an electric heat source. Both are good for slow cooking stews and soups. Simply add the ingredients to these cookers and turn the temperature dial to the appropriate setting. Six to eight hours later, the meal is ready. More information on crockpots and slow-cookers is found in Chapter 4, Stews, beginning on page 67.

Steamers

When vegetables are boiled, most of their nutrients are cooked away. On the other hand, steaming vegetables not only prevents this loss of vitamins and minerals, it also helps the vegetables retain their bright color and crispness. Metal steamer baskets with collapsible sides and vent holes fit inside pots. They are inexpensive and can be purchased in any store that sells kitchen gadgets.

Microwave-Safe Dishes

For those of us who simply don't have the hours to spend toiling over a stove while the vegetables sauté or the potatoes bake, the microwave oven can be a real salvation. Many of my recipes can be easily prepared in the microwave. Using the microwave not only speeds up cooking time, it also makes certain preparation methods, such as sautéing vegetables, a thing of the past. Instead of taking extra time and adding extra calories and fat by sautéing vegetables in a skillet, I simply place a tablespoon of water in a microwave-safe bowl, add the vegetables, cover with wax paper, and cook in the microwave for 3 to 4 minutes on high power.

If you prefer to use the stovetop or the oven when cooking foods, that's fine too. But, if time is a precious commodity, and you plan on using your microwave, be sure to have a few microwave-safe bowls and dishes on hand.

NUTRITIONAL ANALYSIS

The nutritional analysis for the recipes in this cookbook was calculated using Master Cook Cooking Light by Sierra On-line, Inc. Product information from manufacturers and the United States Department of Agriculture was also used.

You may find that some of the recipes list optional ingredients. For example, a recipe may give you a choice between ground turkey and vegetable protein crumbles. This option has been given so you can create dishes that suit your taste. The nutritional analysis is always based on the first ingredient listed.

THINK "FAT-FREE"

Remember, you don't have to sacrifice flavor to save calories and lower fat content. And the recipes in the following chapters will prove it to you.

Try reducing the fat in your diet as a personal challenge. Start thinking "fat-free." Think of fat-free mayonnaise and salad dressings instead of the full-fat varieties. Think of nonfat yogurt or nonfat sour cream instead of regular sour cream. Choose lean meats and poultry over the more fatty varieties. Eliminate salt and salt-laden products from your diet. Herbs and spices add wonderful flavor to foods, eliminating the need for salt. Remember to always read labels on fat-free products—they are often high in sugar or sodium. And keep an eye out for the myriad of fat-free kosher products that are continuing to become available. They will permit you to expand your dietary choices while conforming to the laws of kosher cooking.

2.
Appetizers

Think of a first course, or appetizer, as a delicious prelude to the rest of the meal. This opening act should stimulate the appetite and make one eager for the meal that follows. An appetizer can be as simple as a plate of sweet melon slices crowned with ripe juicy berries, or as elaborate as a tasty artichoke stuffed with seasoned bread crumbs. In addition to providing first courses to meals, the appetizers in this chapter can easily serve as cocktail party fare, buffet table additions, and simple snacks to enjoy at any time.

For those special dinner parties, consider stimulating your guests' appetites with a tantalizing Seafood Cocktail or a plate of savory Stuffed Mushrooms, and be sure to try the Easy Homemade Gefilte Fish for your Sabbath dinners. At cocktail parties, your guests will enjoy topping their favorite unsalted crackers with such tasty spreads as Vegetarian Chopped Liver, Aunt Katie's Chopped Herring, and creamy Caviar Spread. And watch how quickly the Fresh Homemade Salsa disappears when surrounded by crisp baked corn chips. Planning a buffet? Be sure to include such sensational appetizers as David's Spicy Burritos, plump Potato Pierogen, and Quick-n-Easy Pasta Bean Tuna. And don't forget to serve a platter of spicy Buffalo Wings during those Sunday afternoon football games—they are perfect together.

No matter which appetizer you choose from this chapter, no matter what the occasion, remember that each and every dish is tasty and easy to make. And most important, as an added bonus, they are practically fat-free!

Easy Homemade Gefilte Fish

Yield: *10 servings*

6 cups water

3 large onions, peeled

3 small carrots, peeled

FISH BLEND

2 pounds white fish fillets, such as flounder, cod, or haddock, cut into cubes

$\frac{1}{2}$ cup water

4 medium egg whites

$\frac{1}{2}$ cup unsalted matzoh meal

1 large onion, finely chopped

$\frac{1}{2}$ teaspoon ground white pepper

Usually served chilled, this blend of finely chopped white fish, matzoh meal, and seasonings tastes even better when it is refrigerated for 8 hours or overnight. Serve with horseradish on the side.

1. Bring the water to boil in a large saucepan. Add the whole onions and carrots, and return to a boil; cook for 15 minutes.

2. To make the fish blend, add the cubed fish, one cup at a time, to a food processor, and process until finely ground. Add the water, egg whites, matzoh meal, chopped onion, and pepper to the food processor, and continue to process for 10 seconds to blend the ingredients well.

3. Shape this mixture into approximately 10 oval balls.

4. Remove the carrots and onions from the saucepan, discard the onion, and reserve the carrots. Gently place the fish balls in the water, reduce the heat to medium, and cook for 40 minutes, or until the middle of the balls are completely white.

5. Remove the balls from the water and place in a heatproof bowl. Pour the cooking water on top, cover the bowl, and refrigerate.

6. Serve the gefilte fish chilled and topped with slices of the cooked carrot.

NUTRITIONAL FACTS (PER SERVING)
Calories: 107   Carbohydrates: 8.4 g   Cholesterol: 0 mg
Fat: 0.6 g   Fiber: 0.8 g   Protein: 15.9 g   Sodium: 140 mg

Seafood Cocktail

This tasty appetizer is quick and easy to prepare. Feel free to substitute the cocktail sauce with a low-sodium commercial variety.

1. Bring the water to boil in a 2-quart saucepan. Add the fish fillets and onion and return to a boil. Cook the fish about 10 minutes, or until tender. Remove and discard the onion.

2. Transfer the fish to a bowl, cover, and refrigerate for 30 minutes. Cut the cooled fillets into small cubes.

3. To make the cocktail sauce, combine the salsa and horseradish in a small bowl.

4. Divide the fish on individual dishes, top with cocktail sauce, and serve.

Yield: *6 servings*

4 cups water

8 ounces cod or halibut fillets

1 large onion, peeled and left whole

COCKTAIL SAUCE

¼ cup mild low-sodium salsa or ketchup

2 tablespoons horseradish

NUTRITIONAL FACTS (PER SERVING)
Calories: 37   Carbohydrates: 4.3 g   Cholesterol: 16 mg
Fat: 0.3 g   Fiber: 0.1 g   Protein: 6.8 g   Sodium: 72 mg

Vegetarian Chopped Liver

This vegetarian chopped liver tastes like the real thing.

1. Heat the oil in a small nonstick skillet over medium-low heat. Add the onion, and sauté until soft and beginning to brown.

2. Drain the onion on paper toweling, then place in a blender or food processor along with the remaining ingredients. Process until well-blended.

3. Serve with melba toast rounds or your favorite unsalted crackers.

Yield: *2 cups*

1 teaspoon olive oil

1 large onion, coarsely chopped

3 medium hard-boiled egg whites

12-ounce can green beans, drained

2 slices pumpernickel bread, cut into quarters

5-ounce can shelled walnuts

NUTRITIONAL FACTS (PER TABLESPOON)
Calories: 18   Carbohydrates: 2.1 g   Cholesterol: 0 mg
Fat: 0.8 g   Fiber: 0.4 g   Protein: 1 g   Sodium: 36 g

Grandma Bertha's Mushrooms and Onions

Yield: *6 servings*

2 cups fresh white mushrooms

2 medium Vidalia or other sweet onions, finely chopped

1 teaspoon water

1 teaspoon paprika

I sometimes use shiitake or Portabella mushrooms to give this old family favorite a contemporary touch.

1. Clean the mushrooms and cut them into 1-inch slices.

2. Spray a large nonstick skillet with olive oil cooking spray and place over medium heat. Add the mushrooms, onions, water, and paprika, and cook about 10 minutes, or until the vegetables are tender.

3. Serve hot as a topping on toasted bread or unsalted crackers.

NUTRITIONAL FACTS (PER SERVING)
Calories: 22   Carbohydrates: 4.7 g   Cholesterol: 0 mg
Fat: 0.2 g   Fiber: 1.6 g   Protein: 1.4 g   Sodium: 9 mg

Caviar Spread

Yield: *8 servings*

3 ounces whipped fat-free cream cheese

1 tablespoon fat-free sour cream

2 hard-boiled medium egg whites, finely chopped

1 medium Vidalia or other sweet onion, finely chopped

1 ounce black kosher caviar

Kosher caviar typically comes from whitefish and other kosher-certified fish.

1. In a medium bowl, combine the cream cheese and sour cream until well blended. Add the egg whites and onion and mix well. Gently fold in the caviar.

2. Cover and refrigerate until chilled.

3. Serve with melba toast rounds or unsalted crackers.

NUTRITIONAL FACTS (PER SERVING)
Calories: 32   Carbohydrates: 2.5 g   Cholesterol: 23 mg
Fat: 0.7 g   Fiber: 0.5 g   Protein: 3.7 g   Sodium: 130 mg

Iced Caviar

This appetizer is the perfect opening act for that special dinner party.

Yield: *6 servings*

1. Finely chop the egg whites and place them in a small bowl. Finely chop the onion and place it in another small bowl.

2. Spoon the caviar into a small glass bowl and place it in a larger bowl that is filled with crushed ice.

3. Arrange the three bowls in the center of a large platter that is filled with melba toast rounds or unsalted crackers. Top the crackers with a little caviar, egg white, and onion, and enjoy.

1 ounce black or red kosher caviar

2 hard-boiled medium egg whites

1 medium Vidalia or other sweet onion

NUTRITIONAL FACTS (PER SERVING)
Calories: 25   Carbohydrates: 2 g   Cholesterol: 28 mg
Fat: 0.9 g   Fiber: 0.6 g   Protein: 2.8 g   Sodium: 93 mg

Aunt Katie's Chopped Herring

My Great Aunt Katie made this dish every week until she was well into her nineties.

Yield: *1 cup*

1. Add the herring and egg whites to a food processor and process until finely ground. Transfer to a bowl.

2. Add the apple and onion to the food processor and process until finely ground, then add the fish mixture. Process until all the ingredients are well-combined.

3. Place the mixture in a covered bowl and refrigerate until chilled.

4. Serve as a topping on unsalted crackers.

6-ounce jar herring in wine sauce

2 hard-boiled medium egg whites

1 medium apple, peeled, cored, and sliced

1 medium Vidalia or other sweet onion, sliced

NUTRITIONAL FACTS (PER TABLESPOON)
Calories: 43   Carbohydrates: 3.3 g   Cholesterol: 2 mg
Fat: 2.2 g   Fiber: 0.5 g   Protein: 2.4 g   Sodium: 115 mg

Potato Knishes

Yield: *15 knishes*

Serve these delicious knishes with mustard on the side.

DOUGH

2 packages dry yeast (¼ ounce each)

2 tablespoons warm water

2 cups unbleached all-purpose flour

¼ cup pear baby food

1 medium egg white, unbeaten

¼ cup granulated sugar

1 medium egg white, beaten

FILLING

3 large baking potatoes, peeled and cut into chunks

1 medium onion, cut into chunks

2 medium egg whites

¼ teaspoon ground black pepper

1. Combine the yeast and warm water in a small bowl and let it stand until foamy (about 5 minutes).* If the water does not foam, you can be sure the yeast is past its prime and will not cause the dough to rise. Discard it and begin again with fresh yeast.

2. In a small bowl, blend together the pears and ¼ cup of the flour and set aside. Combine the remaining flour and sugar in a large bowl. Add the yeast and the unbeaten egg white, and blend well. Add the pear mixture and knead into a ball. Cover with plastic wrap and refrigerate 5 to 6 hours (may be refrigerated overnight).

3. Preheat the oven to 350°F. Coat 2 large cookie sheets with cooking spray and set aside.

4. Add alternating chunks of potatoes and onion to a food processor and process until smooth. Transfer this mixture to a fine mesh strainer to drain the excess liquid, then place in a large bowl. Add the remaining filling ingredients and mix well.

5. On a floured board, roll out the dough to a ¼-inch thickness. Using a sharp knife, cut the dough into 4-x-5-inch rectangles, and place 1 tablespoon of filling in the center of each. Fold the right and left sides over the filling, then fold up the remaining sides so they overlap. Press the edges to seal. (*See* Forming a Knish on the next page.)

6. Place the knishes on the cookie sheets, brush with the beaten egg white, and bake for 15 to 20 minutes or until lightly browned.

7. Allow to cool before serving.

* Be sure to use warm water only when checking (proofing) the yeast. If the water is too hot, it will kill the yeast. If the water is too cold, the yeast will work too slowly.

NUTRITIONAL FACTS (PER KNISH)
Calories: 99   Carbohydrates: 20.5 g   Cholesterol: 0 mg
Fat: 0.2 g   Fiber: 0.8 g   Protein: 3.4 g   Sodium: 53 mg

VARIATIONS

- To make kasha knishes, use only 2 potatoes and add 1 cup cooked kasha to the filling mixture.

- For a quick and easy filling, use 1 tablespoon vegetable protein crumbles per knish.

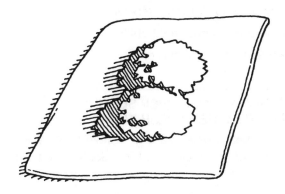

1. *Place the filling in the center of the dough.*

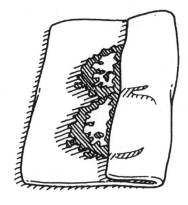

2. *Fold the right and left sides over the filling.*

3. *Fold up the remaining sides so they overlap.*

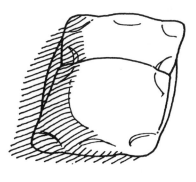

4. *Press the edges to seal.*

Forming a Knish

Quick-n-Easy Pasta Bean Tuna

Yield: *10 servings*

8 ounces fresh tuna fillet, poached (*see* page 134 for poaching instructions)

16-ounce can red kidney beans, drained

2 cups cooked spaghetti

1 tablespoon brown mustard

1 tablespoon fat-free mayonnaise

2 tablespoons fresh tarragon

In a hurry? You can substitute the fresh tuna with a 6-ounce can of chunk light tuna in water for this tasty appetizer.

1. Cut the poached tuna into small chunks and place it in a large bowl. Add the beans and spaghetti, and gently stir to combine. Add the mustard, mayonnaise, and tarragon. Mix well.

2. Cover the mixture and refrigerate until chilled.

3. Spoon onto individual plates and serve.

NUTRITIONAL FACTS (PER SERVING)
FOR POACHED FRESH TUNA

Calories: 159   Carbohydrates: 23.8 g   Cholesterol: 9 mg
Fat: 1.8 g   Fiber: 3.8 g   Protein: 11.7   Sodium: 44 mg

NUTRITIONAL FACTS (PER SERVING)
FOR CANNED TUNA IN WATER

Calories: 154   Carbohydrates: 23.8 g   Cholesterol: 7 mg
Fat: 0.8 g   Fiber: 3.2 g   Protein: 12.2 g   Sodium: 113 mg

David's Speedy Burritos

This dish is a wonderful way to use leftover chulent, which closely resembles the filling of traditional burritos.

1. In a medium bowl, combine the chulent, salsa, and red pepper.

2. Place the tortillas on a clean flat surface. Spoon 2 tablespoons of the mixture along the center of each. Fold the right and left sides of each tortilla about 1 inch over the filling. Then, beginning at the bottom, roll up the tortillas. (*See* Forming a Burrito below.)

3. Place the tortillas seam side down in a microwave-safe baking dish, cover with wax paper, and microwave for 5 minutes on High. Or place the tortillas in an ovenproof dish and bake covered in a 350°F oven for about 10 minutes, or until hot.

4. Serve the burritos with extra salsa and a fresh green salad.

Yield: 6 Burritos

1 cup Tex-Mex Chulent (page 90)*

1 tablespoon mild salsa

¼ teaspoon crushed red pepper flakes

6 fat-free flour tortillas (8 inch)

* Can also use 1 cup cooked ground turkey or vegetable protein crumbles that have been flavored with 2 teaspoons Mexican seasoning mix.

NUTRITIONAL FACTS (PER BURRITO)
Calories: 85 Carbohydrates: 13 g Cholesterol: 0 mg
Fat: 0.1 g Fiber: 7.1 g Protein: 3.1 g Sodium: 185 mg

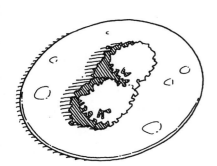

1. Spoon the filling mixture along the center of the tortilla.

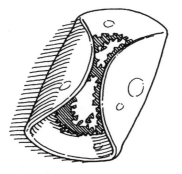

2. Fold the right and left sides over the filling.

3. Roll up the tortilla.

Forming a Burrito

David's Spicy Burritos

Yield: *10 Burritos*

2 cups cooked red kidney beans or chili beans, rinsed and drained

8-ounce can no-sodium tomato sauce

1 medium Vidalia or other sweet onion, coarsely chopped

1 small jalapeño pepper, seeded and chopped

¼ teaspoon chili powder

2 drops hot pepper sauce

10 fat-free flour tortillas (8 inch)

Warning: These three-alarm burritos are very hot and very spicy!

1. Spray a large nonstick skillet with olive oil cooking spray. Add the beans, tomato sauce, onion, and jalapeño pepper, and place over medium heat. Stir in the chili powder and pepper sauce, and mix well. Cook for 10 minutes.

2. Place the tortillas on a clean flat surface. Spoon 2 tablespoons of the bean mixture along the center of each. Fold the right and left sides of each tortilla about 1 inch over the filling. Then, beginning at the bottom, roll up the tortillas. (*See* Forming a Burrito on page 27.)

3. Place the tortillas seam side down in a microwave-safe baking dish, cover with wax paper, and microwave for 5 minutes on High. Or place the tortillas in an ovenproof dish and bake covered in a 350°F oven for about 10 minutes or until hot.

4. You can serve the burritos as is, or top them with salsa.

NUTRITIONAL FACTS (PER BURRITO)
Calories: 141   Carbohydrates: 28.1 g   Cholesterol: 0 mg
Fat: 0.3 g   Fiber: 11.5 g   Protein: 7.4 g   Sodium: 190 mg

Preparing Dried Beans

There are literally hundreds of dried bean varieties. These beans, or legumes, are rich in protein, iron, calcium, and B vitamins. They are also high in fiber, contain zero cholesterol, and are practically fat-free. While beans come in many different shapes and sizes, the methods used to presoak and cook them are similar. Although water amounts and cooking times may vary slightly, the following general guidelines can be applied when preparing most dried beans:

- Always pick through the dried beans for any debris, discolored beans, or empty shells. The beans should then be placed in a colander and rinsed.

- As a general rule, add at least 3 cups of water for every cup of dried beans during cooking. One cup of most bean varieties expands to about 2½ cups cooked.

- When cooking the beans, do not boil them furiously. This will cause their skins to break, resulting in mushy, unattractive beans.

PRESOAKING

With the exception of lentils and split peas, it is a good idea (but not necessary) to presoak dried beans, which cuts down on their cooking time. Basically, there are three presoaking methods:

1. Place the beans in a bowl, cover with water, and soak in the refrigerator for 8 hours or overnight. Drain and rinse the beans before cooking them.

2. Place the beans in a large pot along with 3 cups of water for every cup of beans. Bring to a boil and cook for 2 minutes. Remove the pot from the heat, cover, and let the beans soak for 30 minutes. Drain and rinse the beans before cooking them.

3. Place the beans in a microwave-safe bowl and cover with water. Microwave for 4 to 7 minutes on High. Drain and rinse the beans before cooking them.

COOKING METHODS

When cooking most dried bean varieties, I always choose one of the following methods:

1. Place the rinsed beans in a large pot and add 3 cups of water for every cup of beans. Bring to a boil, then reduce the heat to medium-low. Cover the pot and simmer the beans gently until they are tender, stirring once or twice. This cooking method may take anywhere from 30 minutes to 3 hours depending on the size and type of bean, and whether or not the beans were presoaked.

2. To microwave, place the rinsed beans in a microwave-safe bowl. Add 3 cups of water for every cup of beans. Place the bowl in the microwave, cover with wax paper, and cook on High for 30–35 minutes. If the beans are not cooked, continue cooking them another 5 minutes, or until they are soft and tender.

Karen's Tasty Artichokes

Yield: *4 artichokes*

4 medium artichokes

¾ cup seasoned bread crumbs
(3 tablespoons per artichoke)

1 teaspoon olive oil (¼
teaspoon per artichoke)

To eat these delicious artichokes, remove one leaf at a time and pull it across your bottom teeth to remove the tender "meat." Discard the remaining tough part of the leaf. Sometimes, the inner leaves of an artichoke are so tender they can be eaten in their entirety. Just remember not to eat the choke—the innermost purple-tipped, thorny leaves. Remove the choke with a spoon or fork to get to the delicious artichoke heart.

1. To prepare the artichokes for cooking, cut off their stems with a serrated knife. Place each artichoke on its side and slice about 1 inch off the top. With a kitchen scissors, snip off the thorny ends of each leaf.

2. In a large pot, stand the artichokes upright. Add enough water to cover the bottom half the artichokes. Cover the pot, bring the water to a boil, and cook the artichokes for about 30 minutes or until they are tender. To test for doneness, gently pull one of the inner leaves from the artichoke. If the leaf comes out easily, the artichoke is tender enough to eat.

3. Using a pair of tongs or a large spoon, remove the artichokes from the pot and place them on a clean work surface. When they are cool enough to handle, spread the leaves apart as much as possible, and place them in a microwave-safe baking dish.

4. Sprinkle ¼ teaspoon of olive oil over each artichoke, then add 3 tablespoons of bread crumbs to each. Try to get as much of the oil and bread crumb as possible on the inside of the leaves.

5. Place in the microwave and cook for 3 minutes on High. Or bake in a 350°F oven for 8 to 10 minutes until the artichokes are hot.

6. Serve hot, warm, or at room temperature.

NUTRITIONAL FACTS (PER ARTICHOKE)

Calories: 76   Carbohydrates: 17.4 g   Cholesterol: 0 mg
Fat: 0.6 g   Fiber: 6.9 g   Protein: 4.7 g   Sodium: 220 mg

Stuffed Mushrooms

An elegant tasty appetizer for any dinner party.

1. Preheat the oven to 350°F. Spray a medium baking dish with olive oil cooking spray and set aside.

2. In a bowl, combine the ground turkey, tomato sauce, and bread crumbs. Spoon 1 tablespoon of this mixture into each mushroom cap, then place in the baking dish.

3. Bake uncovered for 20 minutes, or until the turkey is no longer pink.

4. Place the mushrooms on a serving dish. Enjoy hot or cold.

Yield: *12 mushrooms*

12 large fresh white mushrooms, stems removed

8 ounces ground white meat turkey

2 tablespoons no-sodium tomato sauce

2 tablespoons seasoned bread crumbs

NUTRITIONAL FACTS (PER MUSHROOM)
Calories: 25   Carbohydrates: 1.8 g   Cholesterol: 8 mg
Fat: 0.3 g   Fiber: 0.2 g   Protein: 3.7 g   Sodium: 43 mg

VARIATION

• For a vegetarian version, replace the turkey with 4 ounces of vegetable protein crumbles. Bake until the crumbles are soft.

NUTRITIONAL FACTS (PER MUSHROOM)
WITH VEGETABLE PROTEIN CRUMBLES
Calories: 24   Carbohydrates: 3.1 g   Cholesterol: 0 mg
Fat: 0.1 g   Fiber: 0.8 g   Protein: 2.8 g   Sodium: 76 mg

Potato Pierogen

Yield: 15 pierogen

DOUGH

1 cup all-purpose unbleached flour

1 medium egg white

2 tablespoons cold water

FILLING

2 medium baking potatoes, peeled and cut into chunks

1 small onion, cut into chunks

1 medium egg white

¼ teaspoon ground black pepper

These potato-filled pierogen are plump and delicious. The variations below provide a number of filling options.

1. To make the dough, combine the flour and egg white in a medium bowl. Slowly add the cold water while stirring, and continue mixing until the dough is stiff. Knead the dough for 5 minutes until smooth and shiny. Form into a ball and cover in plastic wrap or place in a sealed storage bag. Refrigerate for 1 hour.

2. To make the filling, add alternating chunks of potatoes and onion to a food processor and process until smooth. Transfer this mixture to a fine mesh strainer to drain the excess liquid, then place in a large bowl. Add the remaining filling ingredients and mix well.

3. Bring a large pot of water to a rapid boil.

4. While the water is heating up, roll out the chilled dough to a ¼-inch thickness. Using a round cookie cutter or water goblet, cut the dough into 3-inch circles and place a teaspoon of filling in the center of each. Wet the edges of the circles, fold them in half, and pinch the edges together tightly. (*See* Forming Pierogen below.)

Forming Pierogen

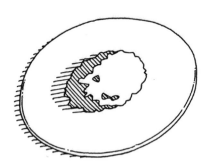

1. Place the filling in the center of the dough.

5. Drop the filled dough into the boiling water and cook for 5 minutes. They will almost double in size and float to the top when ready. Remove with a slotted spoon.

6. Serve the pierogen hot. They are delicious with applesauce or fat-free sour cream.

NUTRITIONAL FACTS (PER PIEROGEN)

Calories: 46   Carbohydrates: 9.5 g   Cholesterol: 0 mg
Fat: 0.1 g   Fiber: 0.4 g   Protein: 1.7 g   Sodium: 45 mg

VARIATIONS

- For meat- or vegetable protein-filled pierogen, use the filling called for in Kreplach recipe on page 46.
- For dairy pierogen, use the filling used in the Cheese Blintzes on page 208 (use ¼ of the ingredient amounts called for).

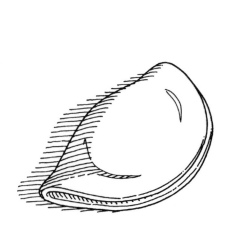

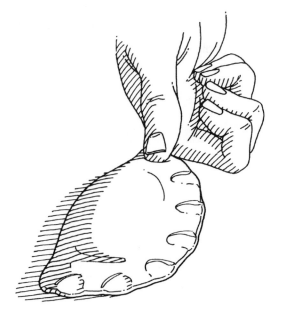

2. Wet the edges of the dough and fold in half.

3. Press the edges together to seal.

Fresh Homemade Salsa

Yield: *2 cups*

4 medium-sized ripe tomatoes, cut into chunks

1 small onion, halved then quartered

1 medium green bell pepper, seeded and sliced

1 small jalapeño pepper, seeded

1 small green chile pepper, seeded

3 medium carrots, peeled and cut in thirds

1 garlic clove, cut in half

This zesty fresh salsa is a great dip for raw vegetables and low-fat chips. You can also use it in recipes such as Tex Mex Chulent (page 90) and Thirty-Second Salsa Chicken (page 103).

1. Place all of the ingredients in a food processor or blender and process for 5 to 10 seconds. The mixture should be somewhat chunky.

2. Serve at room temperature or chilled.

3. Stored in a tightly sealed container and refrigerated, this salsa will keep for 2 weeks.

NUTRITIONAL FACTS (PER ¼-CUP SERVING)

Calories: 36   Carbohydrates: 8.3 g   Cholesterol: 0 mg
Fat: 0.3 g   Fiber: 2.1 g   Protein: 1.4 g   Sodium: 84 mg

Buffalo Wings

Serve these tasty wings as appetizers or snacks. They make great Superbowl party fare.

Yield: *8 servings*

1 pound chicken wings

1/4 cup Spicy Barbecue Sauce (page 87), or commercial variety

1/4 cup water

1 teaspoon white vinegar

1. Preheat the oven to 350°F. Spray a 9-x-13-inch baking dish with olive oil cooking spray.

2. Wash the chicken wings and remove as much of the skin and excess fat as possible. Separate the wings at the joints and discard the small tips.

3. In a bowl, combine the barbecue sauce, water, and vinegar.

4. Place the wings in a single layer in the baking dish and coat lightly with the sauce mixture.

5. Bake for 30 minutes, or until wings are no longer pink inside.

6. Pile the wings onto a platter and serve.

NUTRITIONAL FACTS (PER SERVING)
Calories: 44   Carbohydrates: 1 g   Cholesterol: 17 mg
Fat: 1.2 g   Fiber: 0.1 g   Protein: 6.8 g   Sodium: 88 mg

Cold Sesame Noodles

Yield: *8 servings*

8 ounces spaghetti

1 tablespoon reduced-fat
  smooth peanut butter

1 teaspoon low-sodium soy
  sauce

¼ cup water

1 teaspoon sesame seeds

1 medium scallion, white and
  light green part only, thinly
  sliced

These flavorful noodles are the perfect accompaniment to serve with Peanut Butter Chicken (page 98).

1. Cook the spaghetti al dente according to package directions.

2. While the pasta is cooking, prepare the sauce. In a microwave-safe bowl, combine the peanut butter, soy sauce, and water. Cover the bowl with wax paper, and microwave for 30 seconds on High or until the mixture is hot. Stir the mixture until the ingredients are smooth and well-blended. You can also heat these ingredients in a small saucepan over medium heat.

3. Drain the cooked pasta, rinse with cold water, and drain again. Return the pasta to the pot, add the sauce, and toss to coat. Transfer the spaghetti to a serving dish, top with scallions, and sprinkle with sesame seeds. Cover and refrigerate.

4. Serve chilled.

NUTRITIONAL FACTS (PER SERVING)

Calories: 120   Carbohydrates: 21.5 g   Cholesterol: 0 mg
Fat: 1.4 g   Fiber: 0.9 g   Protein: 4.3 g   Sodium: 35 mg

3.
Soups

There is probably nothing more comforting than the soothing aroma of hot, simmering soup. Delicious and satisfying, soup can be considered a true comfort food—it warms the heart and soothes the spirit. And whether it's clear and light or thick and chunky, soup can be flavorful and satisfying, yet low in fat or even fat-free.

As delicious and heartwarming as soup can be, most meat- and poultry-based varieties can also be full of fat. The good news is that getting rid of this fat is a simple task. While the soup is cooking, periodically skim off the fat that floats to the top. By the time you serve the soup, its fat content will be insignificant. If you are going to serve the soup at a later time or the next day, place the entire pot in the refrigerator. As the soup cools, the fat will rise to the top and harden. You can easily spoon off this layer of fat and discard it before reheating the soup.

SOUP FOR THE SABBATH

I love to serve my guests steaming fragrant bowls of soup at Sabbath meals. Cooking, however, is not permitted on the Sabbath. In order to enjoy hot soup during this time, it must be cooked before Sabbath begins and kept warm throughout. So I either place the cooked hot soup in a crockpot that has been set on Low before the Sabbath begins, or I keep it in a pot that has been placed on a special metal sheet called a *blech*. The blech is set over a stove burner that stays lit during the Sabbath.

When I am going to be serving soup on Friday night only (not during the entire Sabbath), I generally bring the cooked soup to a boil for about five minutes in the late afternoon just before the Sabbath begins. Then I cover the pot and turn off the heat. This keeps the soup hot until it is time for dinner.

On those Fridays when I know I won't be getting home early enough to prepare soup before the Sabbath, I start cooking the soup in a crockpot that morning. The hot, fresh soup is ready by dinner. For cooked soup to remain hot during the Sabbath, I keep it in a crockpot set on Low. This keeps the soup hot without overcooking it. When using this method, I always add a cup of boiling water to the crockpot along with the soup.

SOUP STOCK

A flavorful, rich-tasting stock can provide a flavorful base to a number of soups. It is an important ingredient in many of my recipes. I find that a good stock is especially important in light soups and broths whose main ingredients cannot stand on their own. For thicker, heartier varieties that include strong-flavored vegetables and other ingredients, a stock is not always necessary.

Of course, great-tasting homemade stock is always preferred over commercial brands. To me, the taste of canned stock cannot compare to one made from scratch. As an added bonus, homemade stock allows you to control the quality of the ingredients, as well as the fat and sodium content.

There are, however, a number of fat and sodium-free commercial stocks that are acceptable. When using a canned stock that is not fat-free, place the can in the refrigerator for a few hours. This will cause the fat to rise to the top, making it easy for you to remove it. Dry bouillon is another convenient substitute for homemade stock. However, while bouillon may be fat-free, most varieties are high in sodium. Be sure to read labels and select only low-sodium brands.

Chicken, veal, and fish stocks are used in a number of recipes throughout this book. These basic stock recipes are presented in Savory Soup Stocks beginning on page 39. Whenever I have the time, I prepare a batch of stock, separate it into small containers, then refrigerate or freeze it until needed. This way, I always have delicious stock on hand to use at a moment's notice.

A WORD ABOUT CHICKEN SOUP

Chicken soup is very versatile. It is also the traditional soup for the Sabbath. An endless range of vegetables, grains, and other ingredients can be added to chicken soup for variety. Try adding rice, pasta, barley, or beans to a basic chicken soup recipe for satisfying results; or stir in an egg white for a healthy version of Chinese egg drop soup. These ingredients can add the perfect touch to your already delicious chicken soup, and the possibilities are virtually unlimited.

Chicken soup gets its wonderful aroma, delicious taste, and deep golden color from the chicken. The chicken soup recipes in this chapter call for skinless white meat chicken with the bones. Once the chicken is cooked, you can remove it from the soup, or leave it in during the soup's entire cooking time. The longer the chicken cooks, the richer the soup will be. And don't worry about any leftover soup chicken. Beginning on page 115, there is a variety of recipes that call for this ingredient.

Now, get ready to try a number of delicious fat-free and low-fat soups that include a wide variety of healthful and nutrient-rich ingredients. Combinations of fresh garden vegetables, wholesome grains and beans, and fish, chicken, and other lean meats result in satisfying soups that are further enlivened with the addition of flavorful herbs and spices. Light soups such as Cream of Mushroom-Leek and Two-Minute Cold Cucumber Soup are perfect to serve as introductions to a main meal. More substantial creations like Chicken Broccoli or Black Bean Soup are satisfying main courses for a hearty lunch or a light dinner. And, of course, there are such traditional favorites as Old Fashioned Chicken Soup and Grandma Bertha's Split-Pea Soup that are good to enjoy anytime.

Top Left: *Seafood Cocktail (page 21)*
Top Right: *Karen's Tasty Artichokes (page 30)*
Bottom Left: *Stuffed Mushrooms (page 31)*
Bottom Right: *Easy Homemade Gefilte Fish (page 20)*

Left: Old Fashioned Chicken Soup (page 42) with Guilt-Free Matzoh Balls (page 45)

Top Right: Dried Fruit Tsimmes (page 166)

Bottom Right: Grandma Helen's 90's-Style Hungarian Goulash (page 79)

Savory Soup Stocks

Flavorful, rich-tasting chicken, veal, and fish stocks are called for in a number of recipes throughout this book. Whenever I have the time, I make a batch of stock, separate it into small containers, then refrigerate or freeze it until needed. This way, I always have delicious stock on hand to use at a moment's notice. Stock can be kept in the freezer up to six months. Just remember to leave a small amount of room in the containers to allow for expansion.

Feel free to use the following broths as the base for soups or as a flavor enhancer for other dishes. They are all fat- and sodium-free, and each cup contain less than 20 calories.

Chicken Stock

1. Bring the water to boil in a 6-quart pot. Add the chicken and return to a boil. Add the remaining ingredients, reduce the heat to low, and simmer partially covered for 1 to 2 hours. The longer the soup simmers, the richer the flavor.

2. As the soup simmers, occasionally skim off the fat that rises to the top.

3. Using a slotted spoon, remove all of the ingredients. Reserve the chicken for another use (*see* Recipes for Leftover Soup Chicken beginning on page 115). For a clearer stock, strain the cooled soup through a cheesecloth-lined strainer.

4. Refrigerate the stock for at least 2 hours, then remove and discard any fat that has risen to the top.

5. Use the stock immediately or place it in small containers and store in the freezer where it will keep up to six months.

Yield: *2½ quarts*

4 quarts cold water

3 pounds skinless chicken parts (carcasses from roasted or baked chickens, or any combination of bones, necks, backs, and wings)

2 large onions

4 garlic cloves

2 large sweet potatoes, scrubbed

2 medium tomatoes

3 medium carrots, peeled and quartered

2 parsnips, scrubbed

4 celery ribs, cut into large chunks

6 black peppercorns

4 sprigs fresh parsley

4 sprigs fresh dill weed

2 stems fresh rosemary

2 bay leaves

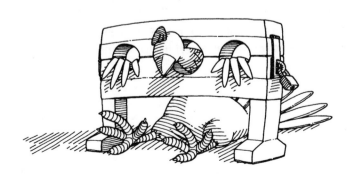

Veal Stock

Yield: *2¹⁄₂ quarts*

4 quarts water

3 pounds veal bones

2 large onions

4 celery ribs, cut into large chunks

4 garlic cloves

4 sprigs fresh parsley

¹⁄₂ teaspoon ground black pepper

1. Bring the water to boil in a 6-quart pot. Add the veal bones to the pot and return to a boil. Add the remaining ingredients, reduce the heat to low, and simmer partially covered for 1½ to 3 hours. The longer the soup simmers, the richer the flavor.

2. As the soup simmers, occasionally skim off the fat that rises to the top.

3. Using a slotted spoon, remove all of the ingredients. For a clearer stock, strain the cooled soup through a cheesecloth-lined strainer.

4. Refrigerate the stock for at least 2 hours, then remove and discard any fat that has risen to the top.

5. Use the stock immediately or place it in small containers and store in the freezer where it will keep up to six months.

Fish Stock

Yield: *2¹⁄₂ quarts*

4 quarts water

2 fish carcasses, including heads

2 large onions

5 medium carrots, peeled and quartered

4 celery ribs, cut into large chunks

4 leeks, sliced

2 parsnips, scrubbed

2 turnips, scrubbed

4 garlic cloves

4 sprigs fresh parsley

4 sprigs fresh dill weed

2 bay leaves

Be sure to use only kosher-certified fish for this stock. And check with your local fish market. They are usually quite happy to give away fish bones. Gills and eyes should be removed.

1. Bring the water to boil in a 6-quart pot. Add the fish carcasses to the pot and return to a boil. Add the remaining ingredients and boil uncovered for 15 minutes. Reduce the heat to low and simmer uncovered for 1 to 3 hours. The longer the soup simmers, the richer the flavor.

2. Using a slotted spoon, remove all of the ingredients. For a clearer stock, strain the cooled soup through a cheesecloth-lined strainer.

3. Use the stock immediately or place it in small containers and store in the freezer where it will keep up to six months.

Chicken Broccoli Soup

Yield: *8 servings*

4 cups homemade Chicken Stock (page 39), or fat-free commercial variety

2 cups water

1 1/4 pounds fresh broccoli, chopped*

1 medium potato, peeled and cubed

1 large onion, coarsely chopped

3 garlic cloves, sliced

1/4 teaspoon ground black pepper

1/8 teaspoon ground nutmeg

* Can use 2 packages (10 ounces each) frozen chopped broccoli, thawed. Add in Step 2.

Rich in vitamin C, beta carotene, bioflavonoids, and calcium, broccoli is one of the cruciferous vegetables, which are known for their cancer-fighting properties.

1. Bring the chicken stock and water to boil in a 4-quart pot. Add the broccoli, potato, onion, and garlic, and return to a boil. Reduce the heat and simmer uncovered for 15 minutes.

2. Add the black pepper and nutmeg. Continue to simmer 30 minutes.

3. Ladle the soup into individual bowls. Serve hot.

NUTRITIONAL FACTS (PER SERVING)
Calories: 37   Carbohydrates: 6.4 g   Cholesterol: 0 mg
Fat: 0.2 g   Fiber: 2.6 g   Protein: 2.4 g   Sodium: 95 mg

Suggested Additions to Basic Soups

Add a little variety to simple basic soup recipes, such as Old Fashioned Chicken Soup (page 42), No-Time-to-Shop Chicken Soup (page 43), and Sweet Ginger Soup (page 49), by including one of the following ingredients:

- *Matzoh balls (recipe on page 45).*
- *Kreplach (recipe on page 46).*
- *No-yolk egg noodles. (Add about 6 minutes before serving.)*
- *Barley. (Add about 30 minutes before serving.)*
- *Egg whites. (Stir into the soup about 5 minutes before serving.)*
- *Rice. (Add white rice about 20 minutes before serving, brown rice about 30 minutes, and wild rice about 40 minutes.*
- *Pasta—any small variety, such as orzo. (Add about 10 minutes before serving.)*

Old Fashioned Chicken Soup

Yield: *10 servings*

Chicken soup is the traditional soup of the Sabbath and most holidays.

8 cups cold water

2 pounds skinless white meat chicken parts

1 large onion, peeled and left whole

1 large onion, chopped

2 cloves garlic

1 large sweet potato, scrubbed

1 medium tomato

1 medium parsnip, scrubbed

3 medium carrots, peeled and quartered

2 celery ribs, cut into chunks

3 black peppercorns

2 sprigs fresh parsley

2 sprigs fresh dill weed

1 stem fresh rosemary

2 bay leaves

1. Bring the water to boil in a 6-quart pot. Add the chicken and return to a boil.

2. Add the remaining ingredients to the pot, reduce the heat to low, and simmer partially covered for 1 to 2 hours. The longer the soup simmers, the richer the flavor.

3. As the soup simmers, occasionally skim off the fat that rises to the top.

4. Using a slotted spoon, remove and discard the bay leaf. Transfer the cooked chicken and vegetables to a platter. Reserve the chicken for another use (*see* Recipes for Leftover Soup Chicken beginning on page 115). Slice the carrot and return to the pot, along with any other cooked vegetables you wish to add.

5. Ladle the soup into individual bowls. Serve hot.

NUTRITIONAL FACTS (PER SERVING)
Calories: 10   Carbohydrates: 2.2 g   Cholesterol: 0 mg
Fat: 0 g   Fiber: 0.6 g   Protein: 15.0 g   Sodium: 13 mg

"Jewish Penicillin"

A number of medical studies indicate that chicken soup, commonly known as Jewish Penicillin, may actually help alleviate the symptoms that accompany the common cold. One study showed that cold sufferers given chicken soup reported a decrease in congestion of nasal passageways as compared to cold sufferers given any other type of soup. What is the therapeutic ingredient in chicken soup? Scientists are actually working on an answer to that question. Just remember, when your grandmother brought you that bowl of steaming chicken soup when you were sick, she was actually practicing medicine.

No-Time-to-Shop Chicken Soup

In the mood for chicken soup but don't have the time to shop for fresh ingredients? The only fresh ingredient you will need for this recipe is the chicken (and you can take one out of your freezer). The other ingredients are likely to be on your pantry shelves.

1. Bring the water to boil in a 6-quart pot. Add the chicken and return to a boil.

2. Add the remaining ingredients to the pot, reduce the heat to low, and simmer partially covered for 1 to 2 hours. The longer the soup simmers, the richer the flavor.

3. As the soup simmers, occasionally skim off the fat that rises to the top.

4. Using a slotted spoon, remove and discard the bay leaf. Transfer the cooked chicken to a platter and reserve for another use (*see* Recipes for Leftover Soup Chicken beginning on page 115).

5. Ladle the soup into individual bowls. Serve hot.

Yield: *10 servings*

8 cups water

2 pounds white meat chicken parts, skin removed

3 tablespoons dried soup green flakes

2 teaspoons minced onion flakes

1 teaspoon garlic powder

1 teaspoon dried parsley

1 teaspoon dried dill weed

1/2 teaspoon dried rosemary

3 black peppercorns

2 bay leaves

NUTRITIONAL FACTS (PER SERVING)
Calories: 10   Carbohydrates: 5.2 g   Cholesterol: 0 mg
Fat: 0 g   Fiber: 0 g   Protein: 0.1 g   Sodium: 13 mg

Mulligatawny

Yield: *10 servings*

8 cups water

1 pound white meat chicken
  parts, skin removed

2 medium onions, sliced

2 medium carrots, peeled and
  quartered

2 celery ribs, coarsely chopped

1 garlic clove, coarsely
  chopped

1 cup cooked brown rice

1 teaspoon ground turmeric

WHOLE-SPICE SACHET*

8 green cardamom pods

3 cloves

10 black peppercorns

1 teaspoon coriander seeds

1/2 teaspoon cumin seeds

* You can use 1 tablespoon curry
  powder instead of the whole-spice
  sachet.

This delicious soup from India is the one Kramer went crazy over in an episode of Seinfeld. Wrapping the spices together in a sachet makes it easier to adjust the flavor of the soup. For a mild spiciness, remove the sachet after the soup has been cooking 30 minutes. For a bolder flavor, let the sachet simmer as long as the soup cooks.

1. To make the sachet, place all of the whole spices in the center of a square piece of cheesecloth or a clean cotton handkerchief. Bring up the sides of the cloth and knot tightly to form a small pouch. Set aside.

2. Bring the water to boil in a 6-quart pot. Add the chicken and return to a boil.

3. Add the onions, carrots, celery, and garlic to the pot. Reduce the heat to low and add the brown rice, turmeric, and the spice sachet. Gently stir the ingredients and cook partially covered for 1 hour.

4. As the soup cooks, occasionally skim off the fat that rises to the top.

5. Using a slotted spoon, remove and discard the sachet. Transfer the chicken to a dish. When the chicken is cool enough to handle, remove and discard the bones, then cut the chicken into small pieces and return it to the pot.

6. Ladle the soup into individual bowls. Serve hot.

NUTRITIONAL FACTS (PER SERVING)
Calories: 108   Carbohydrates: 17.6 g   Cholesterol: 14 mg
Fat: 0.4 g   Fiber: 0.6 g   Protein: 7.6 g   Sodium: 136 mg

Traditional Soup Additions

Light, fluffy matzoh balls and plump, savory dumplings called kreplach are traditionally added to chicken soup. Unfortunately, they are also high in fat and calories. The good news is that the following recipes will allow you to enjoy healthful, delicious versions of these traditional favorites.

Guilt-Free Matzoh Balls

Most matzoh balls are made with oil or margarine, and contain 176 calories and 11.4 grams of fat. Compare them to these "guilt-free" matzoh balls, which have only 83 calories and 0.8 fat grams. That's a big difference! This recipe calls for a whole egg, which is necessary for the balls to retain their shape and texture.

Yield: *8 matzoh balls*

1 cup unsalted matzoh meal

1 tablespoon cornstarch*

$1/2$ cup water

1 medium egg

3 medium egg whites

$1/8$ teaspoon ground black pepper

* Substitute potato starch for use during Passover.

1. In a medium bowl, combine the matzoh meal, cornstarch, water, egg, and egg whites, and mix well. Add the pepper and continue to mix until well-blended.

2. Cover the bowl and refrigerate at least 1 hour.

3. Bring 1 quart of water to a rapid boil. Wet your hands, then pick up a small portion (about $1^1/2$ tablespoons) of the chilled batter and form it into a ball. Continue forming balls with the remaining batter.

4. Gently drop the matzoh balls into the boiling water one at a time. Boil for 20 minutes or until the balls float to the surface.

5. Using a slotted spoon, transfer the matzoh balls to the hot soup and allow 5 to 10 minutes for them to absorb the flavor of the soup.

6. Ladle the hot soup and matzoh balls into individual serving bowls.

NUTRITIONAL FACTS (PER MATZOH BALL)
Calories: 83   Carbohydrates: 14.6 g   Cholesterol: 23 mg
Fat: 0.8 g   Fiber: 0 g   Protein: 3.5 g   Sodium: 28 mg

Kreplach

Yield: *15 dumplings*

DOUGH

1 cup unbleached
   all-purpose flour

1 medium egg white

2 tablespoons cold water

FILLING

8 ounces ground white
   meat turkey

1 small onion, finely
   chopped

1 medium egg white,
   beaten

$1/8$ teaspoon ground white
   pepper

Traditionally, these filled dumplings are added to chicken soup and served on holidays, especially during the meal before the fast of Yom Kippur. Delicious in soup, kreplach also make wonderful appetizers. Once boiled, brown the kreplach in a skillet that has been coated with cooking spray. Serve with mustard or sweet-and-sour sauce.

1. To make the dough, combine the flour and egg white in a medium bowl. Slowly add the water and mix until the dough is stiff. Knead the dough until it is smooth and shiny. Form into a ball and cover in plastic wrap or place in a sealed storage bag. Refrigerate for 1 hour.

2. Coat a nonstick skillet with olive oil cooking spray and place over medium heat. Add the turkey and cook until lightly browned, while stirring to crumble. Drain the excess oil. Transfer the turkey to a medium bowl, add the remaining filling ingredients, and combine well.

3. Bring a large pot of water to a rapid boil.

4. While the water is heating up, roll out the chilled dough until paper thin. Using a sharp knife, cut the dough into 3-inch squares. Place 1 teaspoon of filling in the center of each square. Bring up the sides of the dough and pinch together to form a small pouch. (*See* Forming Kreplach on the next page.)

5. Drop the filled pouches into the boiling water, reduce the heat to low, and simmer for 15 minutes or until just tender. Remove with a slotted spoon and reheat in hot soup.

NUTRITIONAL FACTS (PER DUMPLING)
Calories: 47   Carbohydrates: 6.8 g   Cholesterol: 6 mg
Fat: 0.3 g   Fiber: 0.1 g   Protein: 3.9 g   Sodium: 51 mg

VARIATION

• For a vegetarian kreplach to eat with pareve or dairy meals, substitute the ground turkey with 4 ounces of vegetable protein crumbles. Simply combine the crumbles with the remaining filling ingredients.

NUTRITIONAL FACTS (PER DUMPLING)
WITH VEGETABLE PROTEIN CRUMBLES
Calories: 47   Carbohydrates: 7.8 g   Cholesterol: 0 mg
Fat: 0.1 g   Fiber: 0.6 g   Protein: 3.5 g   Sodium: 96 mg

 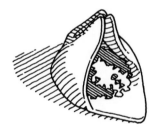 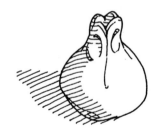

1. Place the filling in the center of the dough.

2. Bring the edges together to form a pouch.

3. Press the edges together to seal.

Forming Kreplach

Autumn Sweet Potato Soup

Yield: *8 servings*

6 cups homemade Chicken
Stock (page 39), or fat-free
commercial variety

1½ pounds sweet potatoes,
peeled and cut into large
chunks

1 medium onion, cut into
quarters

½ teaspoon ground nutmeg

¼ teaspoon ground white
pepper

1 cup Homemade Cranberry
Sauce (page 167), or
8-ounce can commercial
variety (choose whole berry
style)

A wonderfully fragrant soup. Perfect to serve on a brisk fall or winter day.

1. Place the sweet potatoes and onion in a food processor or blender and purée until fine. Set aside.

2. Bring the chicken stock to a boil in a 4-quart pot. Add the sweet potato mixture and return to a boil. Reduce the heat to low, and simmer uncovered for 30 minutes.

3. Stir in the nutmeg and pepper. Continue to simmer another 15 minutes.

4. Place a tablespoon of cranberry sauce in the bottom of each soup bowl and cover with hot soup.

NUTRITIONAL FACTS (PER SERVING)
Calories: 125   Carbohydrates: 26.8 g   Cholesterol: 0 mg
Fat: 0.3 g   Fiber: 2.6 g   Protein: 4.9 g   Sodium: 214 mg

Sweet Ginger Soup

The zing in this soup comes from a tantalizing blend of herbs and spices.

1. Bring the water to boil in a 6-quart pot. Add the chicken and return to a boil.

2. Add the onion, carrots, celery, scallions, and garlic to the pot. Reduce the heat to low, and add the remaining ingredients. Simmer partially covered for 1 to 2 hours. The longer the soup simmers, the richer the flavor.

3. As the soup simmers, occasionally skim off the fat that rises to the top.

4. Using a slotted spoon, remove and discard the bay leaf. Transfer the cooked chicken and vegetables to a platter. Reserve the chicken for another use (*see* Recipes for Leftover Soup Chicken beginning on page 115). Slice the carrot and return to the pot, along with any other cooked vegetables you wish to add.

5. Ladle the soup into individual bowls. Serve hot.

NUTRITIONAL FACTS (PER SERVING)
Calories: 17   Carbohydrates: 3.8 g   Cholesterol: 0 mg
Fat: 0.2 g   Fiber: 0.8 g   Protein: 0.4 g   Sodium: 15 mg

Yield: *10 servings*

8 cups water

2 pounds white meat chicken parts, skin removed

1 medium onion, coarsely chopped

3 medium carrots, peeled and quartered

2 celery ribs, chopped

4 scallions, trimmed and sliced

1 garlic clove, sliced

1 tablespoon brown sugar

1 tablespoon ground ginger

1 teaspoon ground mace

1 teaspoon ground allspice

1 tablespoon chopped dill weed

4 black peppercorns

3 cloves

1 bay leaf

Chopped Turkey Soup

Yield: *10 servings*

Any small pasta may be substituted for the orzo in this recipe.

1 pound ground white meat turkey

1 large onion, coarsely chopped

2 garlic cloves, sliced

6 cups water

28-ounce can no-sodium crushed tomatoes

1 cup orzo, or other small pasta

1/4 teaspoon ground black pepper

1. Coat a large saucepan with olive oil cooking spray and place it over medium heat. Add the turkey, onion, and garlic, and brown about 3 minutes, or until the turkey is no longer pink. Drain the fat.

2. Bring the water to boil in a 4-quart pot. Add the cooked turkey and crushed tomatoes, reduce the heat to low, and simmer uncovered for 30 minutes.

3. Stir in the orzo and black pepper. Simmer uncovered for 25 minutes.

4. Ladle the soup into individual bowls. Serve hot.

NUTRITIONAL FACTS (PER SERVING)

Calories: 98   Carbohydrates: 10.5 g   Cholesterol: 19 mg

Fat: 0.9 g   Fiber: 2.5 g   Protein: 10.1 g   Sodium: 101 mg

VARIATIONS

- For increased flavor and richness, replace the water with 6 cups homemade Veal Stock (page 40) or 1 pound of veal bones.

- Add a 1-cup combination of fresh peas, sliced carrots, and corn kernels to the soup along with the orzo. Add frozen varieties during the last fifteen minutes of cooking time.

Veal Scotch Broth

Reducing the water in this recipe to 4 cups will turn this savory soup into a tasty stew.

Yield: *10 servings*

8 cups water

1 pound veal neck bones

1/2 cup barley, rinsed and drained

1 large onion, sliced

2 celery ribs, coarsely chopped

2 garlic cloves, sliced

8 ounces fresh or canned mushrooms, sliced

3 cloves

1 tablespoon chopped fresh parsley

1 teaspoon ground cumin

1/2 teaspoon ground black pepper

2 bay leaves

1. Bring the water to boil in a 6-quart pot. Trim any excess fat from the veal bones, add the bones to the pot, and return to a boil.

2. Add the barley, onion, celery, garlic, and mushrooms to the pot. Reduce the heat to medium.

3. Add the cloves, parsley, cumin, black pepper, and bay leaves. Cook uncovered for 1 hour.

4. As the soup cooks, occasionally skim off the fat that rises to the top.

5. Using a slotted spoon, remove and discard the bay leaves and cloves. Transfer the veal bones to a plate. When the veal is cool enough to handle, slice the meat off the bones and return it to the pot. Reduce the heat to low, and simmer uncovered another 10 minutes.

6. Ladle the soup into individual bowls. Serve hot.

NUTRITIONAL FACTS (PER SERVING)
Calories: 69   Carbohydrates: 9.1 g   Cholesterol: 10 mg
Fat: 1.6 g   Fiber: 3 g   Protein: 4.4 g   Sodium: 85 mg

Reducing the Fat in Soup

The following guidelines are important in keeping your soups fat-free:

- *Always start with low-fat cuts of poultry or meat, and trim off any excess fat.*
- *Remove the chicken or turkey skin before cooking.*
- *While a meat- or chicken-based soup cooks, periodically spoon off the fat that rises to the top.*
- *Any fat that is present in soup will rise to the surface when it is refrigerated or frozen. Be sure to remove this layer of fat before reheating the soup. For this reason, always store canned soups and stocks in the refrigerator before using.*

Vegetable Fish Broth

Yield: *10 servings*

A light, flavorful broth.

8 cups homemade Fish Stock (page 40)

1 large onion, peeled and left whole

1 large onion, sliced

3 medium carrots, peeled and quartered

2 medium celery ribs, sliced

2 garlic cloves

1 tablespoon fresh dill weed

1 tablespoon chopped fresh parsley

2 bay leaves

1/2 cup orzo or other small pasta

1. Bring the fish stock to boil in a 6-quart pot. Add the onions, carrots, celery, and garlic, and boil uncovered for 15 minutes.

2. Reduce the heat to low and add the dill, parsley, and bay leaves. Simmer partially covered for 1 to 2 hours. The longer the soup simmers, the richer the flavor.

3. Using a slotted spoon, remove and discard the bay leaves. Transfer the vegetables to a platter and either serve them along with the rest of the meal, or add them to the soup.

4. Add the pasta to the pot and simmer uncovered for 25 minutes.

5. Ladle the soup into individual bowls. Serve hot.

NUTRITIONAL FACTS (PER SERVING)
Calories: 27   Carbohydrates: 5.7 g   Cholesterol: 0 mg
Fat: 0.2 g   Fiber: 0.7 g   Protein: 1.2 g   Sodium: 127 mg

VARIATIONS

Feel free to add more vegetables to this soup if you'd like. The following are good choices:

• 2 medium leeks, thoroughly cleaned and cut into large chunks.

• 1 medium parsnip, scrubbed and added whole.

• 1 medium turnip, scrubbed and added whole.

Manhattan Fish Chowder

This tasty soup is similar to the famous Manhattan clam chowder, only with codfish instead of clams.

Yield: *8 servings*

1. Bring the water to boil in a 6-quart pot. Add the codfish and tomato juice. Boil uncovered for 15 minutes.

2. Reduce the heat to low, and add the remaining ingredients to the pot. Simmer partially covered for 1 to 1½ hours. The longer the soup simmers, the richer the flavor.

3. Using a slotted spoon, remove and discard the bay leaf.

4. Ladle the hot soup into individual serving bowls.

NUTRITIONAL FACTS (PER SERVING)
Calories: 93   Carbohydrates: 11.3 g   Cholesterol: 24 mg
Fat: 0.6 g   Fiber: 2.2 g   Protein: 12 g   Sodium: 178 mg

---

2 cups water or homemade Fish Stock (page 40)

1 pound codfish fillets, cubed

5 cups no-sodium tomato juice

1 medium onion, sliced

1 medium green bell pepper, seeded and sliced

2 celery ribs, sliced

1 medium potato, peeled and cubed

1 medium tomato, sliced

1 teaspoon dried soup green flakes

1 tablespoon chopped fresh tarragon

1 teaspoon dried onion soup mix

1 bay leaf

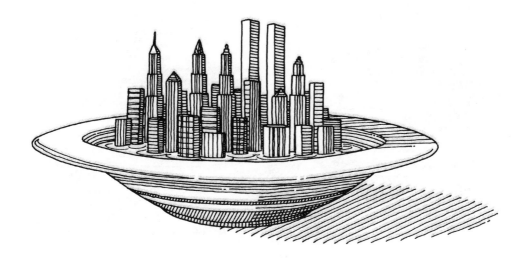

New England Fish Chowder

Yield: *8 servings*

5 cups water

1 pound codfish fillets, cubed

1 medium potato, peeled and
  cubed

1 medium onion, sliced

1½ cups skim milk

16 ounces fresh or frozen peas

¼ teaspoon ground black
  pepper

This kosher version of creamy New England Clam Chowder is a dairy dish.

1. Bring the water to boil in a 6-quart pot. Add the codfish along with the potatoes and onions. Reduce the heat to low, and simmer uncovered for 45 minutes.

2. Stir in the milk, peas, and black pepper, and continue to simmer another 10 minutes.

3. Serve immediately, or refrigerate and enjoy chilled.

NUTRITIONAL FACTS (PER SERVING)

Calories: 121   Carbohydrates: 13.1 g   Cholesterol: 25 mg
Fat: 0.7 g   Fiber: 3.3 g   Protein: 15.1g   Sodium: 131 mg

Riverdale Fish Chowder

While shopping in my neighborhood supermarket, I dreamed up the idea for this soup. I had always wanted to make a thick, rich fish chowder with many different textures. For this recipe, use two or more of the following fish: scrod, whiting, flounder, halibut, or other white fish.

1. Bring the water to boil in a 6-quart pot. Add the fish fillets, return to a boil, and cook uncovered for 15 minutes.

2. Reduce the heat to low and add the remaining ingredients. Simmer partially covered for 1 to 1½ hours. The longer the soup simmers, the richer the flavor.

3. Using a slotted spoon, remove and discard the bay leaves.

4. Ladle the soup into individual serving bowls.

Yield: 10 servings

8 cups water

1½ pounds fish fillets, cut into bite-sized pieces

16-ounce can chick peas, rinsed and drained

16-ounce can peeled white potatoes, rinsed and drained

1 cup fresh or frozen corn kernels

2 medium onions, coarsely chopped

1 garlic clove, sliced

2 scallions, trimmed and chopped

1 cup dry white wine

1 tablespoon Worcestershire sauce

1 tablespoon fresh thyme

1 tablespoon chopped fresh basil

1 teaspoon dried savory

2 bay leaves

NUTRITIONAL FACTS (PER SERVING)
Calories: 115   Carbohydrates: 20 g   Cholesterol: 29 mg
Fat: 0.7 g   Fiber: 1.7 g   Protein: 13.8 g   Sodium: 210 mg

VARIATION

- For added richness, replace 2 cups of the water with homemade Fish Stock (page 40).

A Word About Bay Leaves

Sharp and pungent, bay leaves have been flavoring dishes for centuries. Just be sure to use them sparingly, as one leaf is strong enough to season an entire pot of soup or stew. And remember to remove and discard this inedible leaf before serving the dish.

Grandma Bertha's Split Pea Soup

Yield: *8 servings*

6 cups water

2 cups dried split peas

2 medium carrots, peeled and
   sliced

1 large onion, coarsely
   chopped

4-ounce piece veal brisket,
   turkey pastrami, or turkey
   sausage

$1/8$ teaspoon ground black
   pepper

This was one of my grandmother's favorite soup recipes. I substitute the beef flanken she used with lean veal, turkey pastrami, or turkey sausage.

1. Bring the water to boil in a 4-quart pot. Add the peas, onion, carrots, and veal to the pot, and return to a boil.

2. Reduce the heat to medium, stir in the black pepper, and cook uncovered for $1^{1}/_{2}$ hours or until the meat is tender.

3. Remove the veal from the soup. When it is cool enough to handle, cut the veal into bite-sized pieces and return it to the soup.

4. Ladle the soup into individual bowls. Serve hot.

NUTRITIONAL FACTS (PER SERVING)

Calories: 193   Carbohydrates: 32.3 g   Cholesterol: 8 mg
Fat: 1.3 g   Fiber: 13.4 g   Protein: 14.3 g   Sodium: 96 mg

VARIATION

- If you choose to omit the meat from this soup, you can reduce the fat, calorie, cholesterol, and sodium content even further:

NUTRITIONAL FACTS (PER SERVING)
WITHOUT MEAT

Calories: 179   Carbohydrates: 32.3 g   Cholesterol: 0 mg
Fat: 0.6 g   Fiber: 13.4 g   Protein: 12.4 g   Sodium: 88 mg

Black Bean Soup

Serve this hearty black bean soup with warm crusty bread.

Yield: *8 servings*

1. Bring the water to boil in a 4-quart pot. Add the black beans and return to a boil. Simmer covered for 1½ hours.

2. Add the remaining ingredients to the pot and stir. Simmer covered for 30 minutes.

3. Using a slotted spoon, remove and discard the bay leaf.

4. Ladle the soup into individual bowls. Sprinkle with chopped onion, if desired. Serve hot.

NUTRITIONAL FACTS (PER SERVING)
Calories: 92   Carbohydrates: 17.8 g   Cholesterol: 0 mg
Fat: 0.5 g   Fiber: 4.3 g   Protein: 5.6 g   Sodium: 81 mg

VARIATION

- For a different flavor, add 1 pound of veal bones to the soup. Be sure to skim off any fat that rises to the top as the soup cooks.

6 cups water

1 cup dried black beans, pre-soaked (presoaking instructions on page 29)

1 medium green bell pepper, seeded and chopped

1 medium carrot, sliced

1 celery rib, coarsely chopped

1 large onion, coarsely chopped

1½ teaspoons ground cumin

1 tablespoon chopped fresh parsley

1 bay leaf

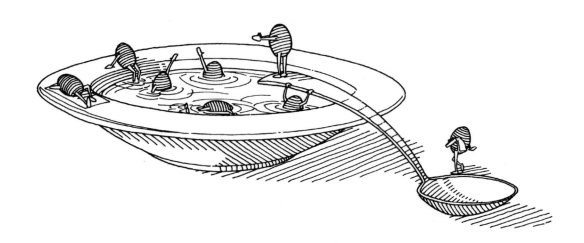

White Bean Soup

Yield: *8 servings*

6 cups water

1 cup dried navy beans, pre-soaked (presoaking instruction on page 29)

1 large onion, finely chopped

1 medium carrot, peeled and sliced

2 celery ribs including leafy tops, cut into chunks

2 tablespoons chopped fresh parsley

1 teaspoon dried savory

¼ teaspoon ground black pepper

2 bay leaves

Purée the beans for a smoother-textured soup.

1. Bring the water to boil in a 4-quart pot. Add the beans and return to a boil. Reduce the heat to low and simmer partially covered for 1 hour.

2. Add the remaining ingredients to the pot and stir. Simmer partially covered for 30 minutes.

3. Using a slotted spoon, remove and discard the bay leaves and celery tops.

4. Ladle the soup into individual bowls. Serve hot.

NUTRITIONAL FACTS (PER SERVING)
Calories: 99   Carbohydrates: 18.4 g   Cholesterol: 0 mg
Fat: 0.4 g   Fiber: 7.1 g   Protein: 6.4 g   Sodium: 93 mg

VARIATIONS

• For added richness, replace 2 cups of the water with homemade Veal Stock (page 40).

• Add 1 pound of veal bones to the soup for a different taste. Be sure to skim off any fat that rises to the top as the soup cooks.

Southern Peanut Soup

An unusual soup with lots of flavor.

Yield: *8 servings*

1. Bring the chicken stock to boil in a 4-quart pot. Reduce the heat to low, add the onion and flour, and stir well. Simmer uncovered for 30 minutes.

2. Stir in the peanut butter, peanuts, and lemon juice. Continue to simmer another 30 minutes.

3. Ladle the soup into individual bowls. Serve hot.

6 cups homemade Chicken Stock (page 39), or fat-free commercial variety

1/4 cup finely chopped onion

2 tablespoons whole wheat flour

2 tablespoons reduced-fat creamy peanut butter

1 tablespoon chopped, roasted unsalted peanuts

1 tablespoon lemon juice

NUTRITIONAL FACTS (PER SERVING)

Calories: 45   Carbohydrates: 1.9 g   Cholesterol: 0 mg
Fat: 2.1 g   Fiber: 0.7 g   Protein: 1.6 g   Sodium: 52 mg

Cream of Mushroom-Leek Soup

Yield: *6 servings*

3 large leeks

2 medium red bell peppers, seeded and sliced

12 ounces mushrooms, sliced

4 cups skim milk

1 tablespoon whole wheat flour

¼ teaspoon ground black pepper

This creamy, flavorful soup is considered dairy. You can enjoy it both hot or chilled.

1. Cut the leeks in half lengthwise and rinse well. Cut away and discard the tough green upper stems. Slice the white and light green parts, and place in a blender or food processor, along with the red peppers, mushrooms, and 2 cups of the milk. Blend about 30 seconds, or until smooth.

2. Add the remaining milk to a saucepan set over low heat and simmer gently. Add the vegetable mixture to the milk. Stir in the flour and black pepper. Simmer 20 minutes.

3. Serve immediately, or refrigerate and serve chilled.

NUTRITIONAL FACTS (PER SERVING)
Calories: 94   Carbohydrates: 17 g   Cholesterol: 3 mg
Fat: 0.6 g   Fiber: 1.7 g   Protein: 7.3 g   Sodium: 92 mg

Cream of Broccoli Soup

This delicious chunky yet creamy soup is considered dairy.

Yield: *8 servings*

1. Bring the water to boil in a 4-quart pot. Add the broccoli, potatoes, onion, and garlic, and return to a boil. Reduce the heat to low and simmer uncovered for 15 minutes.

2. Stir in the milk, flour, black pepper, and nutmeg. Continue to simmer another 20 minutes.

3. Ladle the soup into individual bowls. Serve hot.

NUTRITIONAL FACTS (PER SERVING)
Calories: 78   Carbohydrates: 13 g   Cholesterol: 2 mg
Fat: 0.5 g   Fiber: 2.7 g   Protein: 6.8 g   Sodium: 151 mg

2 cups water

1 1/4 pounds broccoli, finely chopped*

1 medium potato, peeled and cubed

1 large onion, coarsely chopped

3 garlic cloves, sliced

4 cups skim milk

1 tablespoon whole wheat flour

1/4 teaspoon ground black pepper

1/8 teaspoon ground nutmeg

* Can use 2 packages (10 ounces each) frozen chopped broccoli, thawed. Add in Step 2.

Grandma Bertha's Hot Russian Borscht

Yield: *8 servings*

6 medium beets, stems removed and scrubbed well

8 cups water

1 large onion, cut into small chunks

2 garlic cloves, chopped

1/8 teaspoon ground black pepper

1 teaspoon granulated brown sugar

1 teaspoon lemon juice

A warm comforting soup to enjoy on a cold winter day.

1. Place the beets in a large pot and cover with water. Bring to a boil and cook for 20 to 30 minutes or until the beets are just tender. Drain the beets and run under cold water until they are cool enough to handle. Peel off the skins.

2. Bring the 8 cups water to boil in a medium pot.

3. While the water is heating, place the beets, onion, and garlic in a food processor or blender, and process about 30 seconds until the ingredients are mixed yet somewhat chunky.

4. When the water comes to a boil, add the beet mixture, black pepper, brown sugar, and lemon juice. Stir well, reduce the heat to low, and simmer uncovered for 30 minutes.

5. Ladle into bowls and serve hot.

NUTRITIONAL FACTS (PER SERVING)

Calories: 24   Carbohydrates: 5.3 g   Cholesterol: 0 mg
Fat: 0.1 g   Fiber: 1.4 g   Protein: 0.9 g   Sodium: 108 mg

VARIATION

• For a traditional meat borscht, add 4 ounces of veal brisket to the beet mixture in Step 3, and simmer 45 minutes or until tender.

Russian Dairy Borscht

This borscht can be ready in minutes by using canned beets instead of fresh.

Yield: *4 servings*

1. Place the beets in a medium pot and cover with water. Bring to a boil and cook for 20 to 30 minutes, or until the beets are just tender. Drain the beets and run under cold water until they are cool enough to handle. Peel off the skins. Thinly slice one of the beets and set aside.

2. Place the remaining beets in a blender or food processor along with the milk, sour cream, and brown sugar. Blend for 5 to 10 seconds. The beets should be somewhat chunky. Refrigerate until chilled.

3. Spoon the chilled borscht into individual bowls, garnish with beet slices, and serve.

3 medium beets, stems removed and scrubbed well

1 cup skim milk

2 tablespoons fat-free sour cream

1 tablespoon brown sugar

NUTRITIONAL FACTS (PER SERVING)
Calories: 55 Carbohydrates: 10.3 g Cholesterol: 2 mg
Fat: 0.2 g Fiber: 1.2 g Protein: 3 g Sodium: 74 mg

Two-Minute Cold Cucumber Soup

Yield: *4 servings*

2 large cucumbers, unpeeled and cut into thick slices

2 cups nonfat plain yogurt

1 cup skim milk

2 scallions, chopped

½ teaspoon ground white pepper, or ½ teaspoon lemon-pepper seasoning

This dairy soup, which requires no cooking, takes only two minutes to prepare. For a creamier version, peel and seed the cucumbers.

1. Place the cucumbers, yogurt, skim milk, and scallions into a blender or food processor. Blend for 1 minute. Add the white pepper and continue to blend another 10 seconds or until smooth.

2. Refrigerate and serve chilled.

NUTRITIONAL FACTS (PER SERVING)

Calories: 108   Carbohydrates: 16.5 g   Cholesterol: 3 mg
Fat: 0.5 g   Fiber: 1.4 g   Protein: 9.8 g   Sodium: 123 mg

Perl's Purple Fruit Soup

Yield: *8 servings*

28-ounce can peaches in pear juice

12-ounce can plums in light syrup

12-ounce can apricots in light syrup

3 ice cubes

1 cup orange juice

1 teaspoon lemon juice

1 cup halved fresh cherries or sliced peaches

This wonderful light, frothy soup requires no cooking. Canned fruit makes it a snap to prepare.

1. Combine the peaches, plums, and apricots in a large bowl. Place a third of this fruit combination in a blender or food processor along with an ice cube. Blend for 1 minute or until smooth. Transfer this mixture to another large bowl. Repeat with the remaining fruit.

2. Add the orange and lemon juices to the fruit mixture. Mix well, cover, and refrigerate.

3. Serve chilled, topped with cherries or peaches.

NUTRITIONAL FACTS (PER SERVING)

Calories: 111   Carbohydrates: 28.5 g   Cholesterol: 0 mg
Fat: 0.2 g   Fiber: 1.8 g   Protein: 1.4 g   Sodium: 13 mg

No-Cook Cold Strawberry Soup

Another dairy soup that needs no cooking, this cold strawberry soup is perfect on a hot summer day.

Yield: *6 servings*

1. Place the strawberries in a blender or food processor, and purée for 1 minute.

2. Transfer the purée to a large bowl along with the remaining ingredients. Mix well. Cover and refrigerate.

3. Ladle the cold soup into individual serving bowls and garnish with mint.

1 pint ripe strawberries, washed and hulled

2 cups nonfat vanilla yogurt

1 cup orange juice

1 cup white grape juice

1 teaspoon fresh mint leaves (optional)

NUTRITIONAL FACTS (PER SERVING)

Calories: 127   Carbohydrates: 27.1 g   Cholesterol: 1 mg
Fat: 0.4 g   Fiber: 1.2 g   Protein: 4.7 g   Sodium: 54 mg

No-Cook Cold Melon Soup

You can use any type of melon and in any combination when preparing this sensational soup.

Yield: *6 Servings*

1. Cut the melon into chunks and place in a blender or food processor along with the wine, water, and sugar. Blend for 10 seconds, or until very smooth. Cover and refrigerate.

2. Ladle the cold soup into individual serving bowls and garnish with mint.

1/2 medium honeydew (about 1 1/2 pounds), skin removed

1/2 medium cantaloupe (about 1 pound), skin removed

1/2 cup dry white wine

1/2 cup water

2 tablespoons granulated sugar

1 teaspoon fresh mint leaves (optional)

NUTRITIONAL FACTS (PER SERVING)

Calories: 61   Carbohydrates: 12.3 g   Cholesterol: 0 mg
Fat: 0.2 g   Fiber: 0.6 g   Protein: 0.6 g   Sodium: 10 mg

4.

Stews

The Jewish Sabbath begins eighteen minutes before sundown on Friday and ends one hour and ten minutes past sunset on Saturday. It is traditional to serve a hot stew called a chulent on the Sabbath. A chulent includes a mixture of beans and usually some type of meat. As it is customary to eat meat on the Sabbath, many of my stew recipes are made with meat or poultry.

COOKING STEWS

Since it is not permissible to cook on the Sabbath, all foods that are eaten warm should be prepared and cooked at least halfway before sundown on Friday. Then the food needs only to be kept warm throughout the Sabbath. One-piece crockpots, slow-cookers, and blechs are considered acceptable for this purpose. The cooking times listed for the following recipes are the minimums for fully cooking the ingredients. Crockpots and slow-cookers can be set on Low to keep foods warm on the Sabbath without overcooking them.

Crockpots

By maintaining a constant low temperature, crockpots are excellent for keeping most stews and soups warm during the Sabbath. Due to the ingredient choices for the stews in this book, most can be started in a crockpot set to Low on Friday morning, enjoyed Friday night, and still taste good on Saturday afternoon. A stew that is to be served only on Saturday afternoon can be started Friday afternoon and kept warm in the crockpot until it is served. While one-piece crockpots are acceptable, two-piece units are somewhat more controversial. Many rabbinical sources, however, approve of their use (check with your local rabbinic authority).

In addition to keeping food warm during the Sabbath, crockpots are great for making stews any day of the week. Nothing could be easier. In the morning, simply place the ingredients (fresh or frozen) in the crockpot, and turn the setting to Low. Eight hours later, dinner is ready. Sometimes, I add the ingredients to the crockpot the night before, then place the entire crockpot in the refrigerator. Before I leave for work in the morning, I take the crockpot out and plug it in.

Hardy ingredients such as black-eyed peas, wild rice, and barley—foods that can stand up to lengthy cooking times—are good stew choices for crockpot cooking. However, ground meats, boneless cuts of meat, vegetable protein crumbles, texturized vegetable protein, and fish are delicate and tend to break apart in crockpots. Recipes with these ingredients do much better in slow-cookers.

Slow-Cookers

A slow-cooker is a baking dish that rests on a tray with an electric heat source. It is great for keeping foods warm on the Sabbath and for everyday cooking as well. Because a slow-cooker's heat source comes from the bottom only, it will not dry out even the most delicate ingredients. For this reason, ground meats and other ingredients too delicate to hold up in a crockpot, are ideal to use in slow-cookers.

Blechs

Another option for keeping foods warm on the Sabbath is to use a blech. A blech is a sheet of metal that sits on top of the stove's burner. The burner is turned to a very low setting before the Sabbath begins. Hot, cooked food, usually stew or soup, is put into a covered pot and placed on top of the blech. This keeps the food warm throughout the Sabbath. Blechs are sold in many hardware stores.

ABOUT THE STEW RECIPES

All of the stew recipes in this chapter include conventional stovetop cooking instructions. And each recipe, depending upon the nature of its ingredients, also presents simple instructions for preparing the stew in a crockpot or a slow-cooker.

Whenever possible, choose fresh ingredients, which are nutritionally superior to canned or frozen varieties. When necessary, however, you can substitute most of the fresh ingredients called for in the following recipes with those that are canned or frozen. Just be sure to read product nutrition labels carefully. Many canned vegetables have a high sodium content. Choose only unsalted or low-sodium varieties.

Sweet Mustard Chicken Stew

This chicken stew blends the tangy taste of mustard with the hearty goodness of black-eyed peas.

1. Coat a large skillet with olive oil cooking spray and place over medium-low heat. Pat the chicken dry with a paper towel and add to the skillet. Sauté until lightly brown on all sides. Drain any fat from the skillet.

2. Add the remaining ingredients to the skillet and mix well.

3. Cook covered over medium heat for 45 minutes, or until the chicken is no longer pink inside.

4. Transfer the chicken to a serving platter and enjoy with brown rice or thin spaghetti.

CROCKPOT INSTRUCTIONS

1. Rinse and drain the black-eyed peas, then place in a 3-quart crockpot.

2. Add the mustard powder, brown sugar, onion, and parsley. Place the chicken on top of the other ingredients. Add enough water to just cover.

3. Cook on Low setting for 8 to 10 hours.

Yield: *8 servings*

2 pounds skinless chicken breast halves, rinsed and trimmed of any visible fat

16-ounce can black-eyed peas, rinsed and drained*

2 cups water

2 tablespoons mustard powder

2 tablespoons granulated brown sugar

1 large onion, coarsely chopped

1/4 cup chopped fresh parsley

* If using a crockpot, use 1 cup dried black-eyed peas, rinsed and drained.

NUTRITIONAL FACTS (PER SERVING)
Calories: 159   Carbohydrates: 16.7 g   Cholesterol: 36 mg
Fat: 1.7 g   Fiber: 2.5 g   Protein: 19.9 g   Sodium: 119 mg

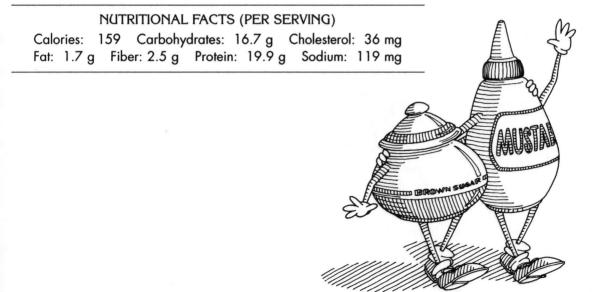

French Herb Chicken Stew

Yield: *6 servings*

2 pounds skinless chicken breast halves, rinsed and trimmed of any visible fat

2 cups dry white wine

1 large onion, coarsely chopped

2 garlic cloves, peeled and left whole

1/4 cup chopped fresh parsley

1/4 cup chopped fresh tarragon

1/4 cup chopped fresh rosemary

2 bay leaves

A light, flavorful herb wine sauce makes this dish a winner.

1. Coat a large skillet with olive oil cooking spray and place over medium-low heat. Pat the chicken dry with a paper towel and add to the skillet. Sauté until lightly brown on all sides. Drain any fat from the skillet.

2. Add the remaining ingredients to the skillet and mix well.

3. Cook covered over medium heat for 45 minutes, or until the chicken is no longer pink inside.

4. Remove the bay leaves before serving.

CROCKPOT INSTRUCTIONS

1. Place all of the ingredients except the chicken in a 3-quart crockpot. Place the chicken on top, and add enough water to just cover.

2. Cook on Low setting for 8 to 10 hours.

NUTRITIONAL FACTS (PER SERVING)

Calories: 186   Carbohydrates: 6.2 g   Cholesterol: 48 mg
Fat: 1.8 g   Fiber: 0.7 g   Protein: 20.2 g   Sodium: 156 mg

Jack's Country Chicken Stew

A wonderful hearty stew.

Yield: *8 servings*

1. Bring 1 cup of water to boil in a small saucepan. Stir in the barley, reduce the heat to medium, and cook for 30 minutes, or until the barley is soft and tender.

2. Coat a large skillet with olive oil cooking spray and place over medium-low heat. Pat the chicken dry with a paper towel, and add to the skillet. Sauté until lightly brown on all sides. Drain any fat from the skillet.

3. Add the barley and the remaining ingredients to the skillet and mix well.

4. Cook covered over medium heat for 45 minutes, or until the chicken is no longer pink inside.

5. Remove the bay leaf before serving.

CROCKPOT INSTRUCTIONS

1. Place all of the ingredients, except the chicken, in a 3-quart crockpot. Place the chicken on top, and add enough water to just cover.

2. Cook on Low setting for 8 to 10 hours.

2 pounds skinless chicken breast halves, rinsed and trimmed of any visible fat

28-ounce can no-sodium crushed tomatoes

½ cup barley, rinsed and drained

1 large onion, coarsely chopped

2 garlic cloves, thinly sliced

8 ounces mushrooms, cut into thick slices

1 tablespoon chopped fresh oregano

1 tablespoon chopped fresh tarragon

1 tablespoon chopped fresh rosemary

1 tablespoon fresh thyme

1 bay leaf

NUTRITIONAL FACTS (PER SERVING)
Calories: 146   Carbohydrates: 16.2 g   Cholesterol: 36 mg
Fat: 1.7 g   Fiber: 4.5 g   Protein: 17.7 g   Sodium: 127 mg

VARIATION

• Sauté 8 ounces of turkey sausage along with the chicken.

Chicken Cacciatora

Yield: *8 servings*

2 pounds skinless chicken breast halves, rinsed and trimmed of any visible fat

8-ounce can no-sodium tomato sauce

1 cup dry red wine

1 cup water

2 medium green bell peppers, seeded and sliced*

2 medium red bell peppers, seeded and sliced*

8 ounces mushrooms, thinly sliced

1 medium onion, thinly sliced

3 garlic cloves, thinly sliced

1 teaspoon chopped fresh oregano

¼ teaspoon ground black pepper

* Can use 8-ounce package frozen bell peppers, thawed and drained.

If you are cooking this dish in a crockpot, add the frozen bell peppers straight from the freezer.

1. Coat a large skillet with olive oil cooking spray and place over medium-low heat. Pat the chicken dry with a paper towel and add to the skillet. Sauté until lightly brown on all sides. Drain any fat from the skillet.

2. Add the remaining ingredients to the skillet and mix well.

3. Cook covered over medium heat for 45 minutes, or until the chicken is no longer pink inside.

4. Place on a platter and serve with warm, crusty bread.

CROCKPOT INSTRUCTIONS

1. Place all of the ingredients, except the chicken, in a 3-quart crockpot. Place the chicken on top, and add enough water to just cover.

2. Cook on Low setting for 8 to 10 hours.

NUTRITIONAL FACTS (PER SERVING)

Calories: 120   Carbohydrates: 6.5 g   Cholesterol: 36 mg
Fat: 1.2 g   Fiber: 1.3 g   Protein: 16.1 g   Sodium: 120 mg

Vegetable Turkey Medley

The lime juice in the marinade tenderizes the turkey and gives it a wonderful tangy flavor.

1. To make the marinade, combine the wine and lime juice in a small bowl.

2. Pat the turkey dry with paper towels and cut it into bite-sized chunks. Place in a glass dish and top with the marinade. Marinate in the refrigerator for at least 30 minutes.

3. Bring 2½ cups of water to boil in a small saucepan. Stir in the rice, reduce the heat to low, and cover. Cook for 35 minutes, or until the rice is tender and easily fluffs with a fork.

4. Coat a large skillet with olive oil cooking spray and place over medium-low heat. Add the rice and top with the turkey pieces.

5. Add the corn, bell peppers, and onion to the skillet. Sprinkle with paprika and garlic powder.

6. Cook uncovered over medium heat for 10 minutes.

7. Transfer to a platter and serve hot.

Slow Cooker Instructions

1. Place all of the ingredients, except the turkey, in a slow cooker. Place the marinated turkey on top, and add enough water to just cover.

2. Cook on Setting 3 for 8 to 10 hours.

Yield: *8 servings*

1 ½-pound turkey London broil

1 cup brown rice

1 cup corn kernels

2 medium red and/or green bell peppers, seeded and chopped

1 small sweet onion, coarsely chopped

1 tablespoon paprika

1 tablespoon garlic powder

MARINADE

½ cup dry white wine

2 tablespoons lime juice

NUTRITIONAL FACTS (PER SERVING)
Calories: 198   Carbohydrates: 28 g   Cholesterol: 36 mg
Fat: 2 g   Fiber: 1.8 g   Protein: 17.7 g   Sodium: 44 mg

Chili con Carne

Yield: *8 servings*

1 pound ground white meat turkey

28-ounce can no-sodium crushed tomatoes

2 cups cooked black beans, navy beans, or black-eyed peas*

2 small jalapeño peppers, finely chopped

1 medium red bell pepper, seeded and chopped

1 medium yellow bell pepper, seeded and chopped

1 large onion, coarsely chopped

1 garlic clove, coarsely chopped

1 teaspoon ground cumin

* If using a slow-cooker, use 1 cup dried beans, rinsed and drained.

The Spanish translation of this recipe title is "Chili with Meat." For a meatless version, see Chili sin Carne (page 76).

1. Coat a large skillet with olive oil cooking spray and place over medium-low heat. Crumble the turkey into the skillet and sauté until brown. Drain any fat from the skillet.

2. Add the tomatoes to the skillet and bring to a boil. Reduce the heat to low and add the remaining ingredients. Mix well.

3. Cover and simmer for 45 minutes.

4. Enjoy as is or spoon into bowls over steaming brown rice.

SLOW-COOKER INSTRUCTIONS

1. Combine all of the ingredients in a slow-cooker and add enough water to just cover.

2. Cook on Setting 3 for 8 to 10 hours.

NUTRITIONAL FACTS (PER SERVING)

Calories: 165   Carbohydrates: 22.9 g   Cholesterol: 24 mg
Fat: 1.4 g   Fiber: 8.7 g   Protein: 16.3 g   Sodium: 110 mg

VARIATION

• For a chili taco, spoon the chili into crisp taco shells, and top with lettuce and diced tomatoes.

Hearty Turkey Stew

Ground turmeric gives this flavorful stew an appetizingly warm color.

Yield: *8 servings*

1. Bring 2½ cups of water to boil in a small saucepan. Stir in the rice, reduce the heat to low, and cover. Cook for 35 minutes, or until the rice is tender and easily fluffs with a fork.

2. Coat a large skillet with olive oil cooking spray and place over medium-low heat. Pat the turkey dry with a paper towel, and add to the skillet. Sauté until lightly brown on all sides. Drain any fat from the skillet.

3. Add the remaining ingredients to the skillet along with the rice, and mix well.

4. Cook covered over medium heat for 1 to 1½ hours.

5. Remove the bay leaves before spooning into bowls and serving.

CROCKPOT INSTRUCTIONS

1. Place all of the ingredients, except the turkey, in a 3-quart crock-pot. Place the turkey on top, and add enough water to just cover.

2. Cook on Low setting for 8 to 10 hours.

1 cup brown rice

2 pounds skinless turkey breasts, cut into large pieces

1 large onion, coarsely chopped

2 garlic cloves, coarsely chopped

1 teaspoon ground turmeric

1 teaspoon ground cumin

2 bay leaves

NUTRITIONAL FACTS (PER SERVING)
Calories: 187   Carbohydrates: 19.3 g   Cholesterol: 48 mg
Fat: 2.1 g   Fiber: 0.5 g   Protein: 21.1 g   Sodium: 123 mg

Chili sin Carne

Yield: *8 servings*

28-ounce can no-sodium
   crushed tomatoes

8 ounces vegetable protein
   crumbles

2 cups cooked black beans,
   navy beans, or black-eyed
   peas*

2 small jalapeño peppers, finely
   chopped

1 medium red bell pepper,
   seeded and chopped

1 medium yellow bell pepper,
   seeded and chopped

1 large onion, coarsely
   chopped

1 garlic clove, coarsely
   chopped

1 teaspoon ground cumin

* If using a slow-cooker, use 1 cup
   dried beans, rinsed and drained.

Vegetable protein crumbles give this hearty chili its meaty texture.

1. Coat a large skillet with cooking spray and place over medium-low heat. Add the tomatoes and bring to a boil. Add the remaining ingredients, and mix well. Reduce the heat to low.

2. Cover and simmer for 30 minutes.

3. Ladle the chili over steaming bowls of brown rice.

SLOW-COOKER INSTRUCTIONS

1. Combine all of the ingredients in a slow-cooker and add enough water to just cover.

2. Cook on Setting 3 for 8 to 10 hours

NUTRITIONAL FACTS (PER SERVING)
Calories: 140   Carbohydrates: 21.7 g   Cholesterol: 0 mg
Fat: 0.6 g   Fiber: 7.7 g   Protein: 13.3 g   Sodium: 278 mg

VARIATION

• For a chili taco, spoon the chili into crisp taco shells, and top with lettuce and diced tomatoes. You can also add shredded low-fat or nonfat cheese if this is a dairy meal.

Cheater's Chili

When you're just too busy to shop, try the following chili recipe. It requires mostly nonperishable ingredients, and can be made on the spur of the moment.

1. Coat a large skillet with olive oil cooking spray and place over medium-low heat. Crumble the turkey into the skillet and sauté until brown. Drain any fat from the skillet.

2. Add the tomatoes to the skillet and bring to a boil. Reduce the heat to low and add the remaining ingredients. Mix well.

3. Cover and simmer for 45 minutes.

4. Spoon into bowls and serve.

SLOW-COOKER INSTRUCTIONS

1. Combine all of the ingredients in a slow-cooker and add enough water to just cover.

2. Cook on Setting 3 for 8 to 10 hours

NUTRITIONAL FACTS (PER SERVING)
Calories: 126   Carbohydrates: 15.1 g   Cholesterol: 24 mg
Fat: 1.2 g   Fiber: 5.7 g   Protein: 14.4 g   Sodium: 42 mg

VARIATION

• For a chili taco, spoon the chili into crisp taco shells, and top with lettuce and diced tomatoes.

Yield: *8 servings*

1 pound ground white meat turkey

28-ounce can no-sodium crushed tomatoes

2 cups cooked black beans, navy beans, or black-eyed peas*

1 teaspoon chili powder

1 teaspoon ground cumin

1/4 teaspoon crushed red pepper flakes

1/2 teaspoon garlic powder

2 drops hot pepper sauce

2 teaspoons dried onion flakes

* If using a slow-cooker, use 1 cup dried beans, rinsed and drained.

Vegetarian Cheater's Chili

Yield: *8 servings*

28-ounce can no-sodium crushed tomatoes

8 ounces protein vegetable crumbles

2 cups cooked black beans, navy beans, or black-eyed peas*

1 teaspoon chili powder

1 teaspoon ground cumin

1/4 teaspoon crushed red pepper flakes

1/2 teaspoon garlic powder

2 drops hot pepper sauce

2 teaspoons dried onion flakes

* If using a slow-cooker, use 1 cup dried beans, rinsed and drained.

A quick and easy meatless chili that is satisfying and delicious.

1. Coat a large skillet with cooking spray and place over medium-low heat. Add the tomatoes and bring to a boil. Add the remaining ingredients and mix well. Reduce the heat to low.

2. Cover and simmer for 30 minutes.

3. Spoon into bowls and serve.

SLOW-COOKER INSTRUCTIONS

1. Combine all of the ingredients in a slow-cooker and add enough water to just cover.

2. Cook on Setting 3 for 8 to 10 hours.

NUTRITIONAL FACTS (PER SERVING)

Calories: 127   Carbohydrates: 18.8 g   Cholesterol: 0 mg
Fat: 0.6 g   Fiber: 7.3 g   Protein: 12.8 g   Sodium: 211 mg

Grandma Helen's 90's-Style Hungarian Goulash

This is the goulash my grandmother would have made if she'd had a microwave and frozen vegetables. It takes only 10 minutes to prepare and 30 minutes to cook.

1. Combine the tomatoes, wine, and brown sugar in a 6-quart pot over low heat. Add the veal, garlic, thyme, savory, paprika, and black pepper. Stir well.

2. Place the potatoes in a microwave-safe bowl. Cover with wax paper and microwave for 5 minutes on High. Add to the pot along with the carrots, green beans, and onion.

3. Increase the heat to medium and cook uncovered for 30 minutes or until the veal is tender.

4. Spoon over broad noodles.

SLOW-COOKER INSTRUCTIONS

1. Place all of the ingredients in a slow-cooker with just enough water to cover. Mix well.

2. Cook on Setting 3 for 8 to 10 hours.

NUTRITIONAL FACTS (PER SERVING)

Calories: 137   Carbohydrates: 10.7 g   Cholesterol: 57 mg
Fat: 2.1 g   Fiber: 2.4 g   Protein: 15.3 g   Sodium: 129 mg

Yields: *10 servings*

16-ounce can no-sodium crushed tomatoes

1 cup dry white wine

2 tablespoons granulated brown sugar

1 garlic clove, thinly sliced

1 teaspoon chopped fresh thyme

1 teaspoon fresh savory

2 tablespoons paprika

1/2 teaspoon ground black pepper

1 1/2 pounds veal stew meat, cut into bite-sized cubes and trimmed of excess fat

2 large potatoes, peeled and cut into bite-sized cubes

1 cup frozen sliced carrots

1 cup frozen sliced green beans

1 large onion, thinly sliced

20-Minute Veal Stew

Yield: *8 servings*

Here's the fastest veal stew east of the Mississippi.

8 ounces linguine

1 cup dry red wine

1 pound veal stew meat, cut into bite-sized cubes and trimmed of excess fat.

2 tablespoons whole wheat flour

2 tablespoons granulated brown sugar

1 medium Vidalia or other sweet onion, coarsely chopped

1 teaspoon, chopped fresh tarragon leaves

1 pinch ground ginger

1. Bring 3 cups of water to boil in a medium saucepan. Add the linguine and cook according to package directions. Rinse, drain, and set aside.

2. Place the flour in a shallow bowl. Dredge the veal cubes in the flour and set aside.

3. While the linguine is cooking, bring the wine to a boil in a large skillet over high heat. Add the veal and the remaining ingredients, and reduce the heat to medium.

4. Cook uncovered for 20 minutes, or until the veal is tender.

5. Place the linguine on a serving platter and top with the veal stew.

SLOW-COOKER INSTRUCTIONS

1. Place all of the ingredients, except the linguine, in a slow-cooker with just enough water to cover. Mix well.

2. Cook on Setting 2 for 6 to 8 hours.

NUTRITIONAL FACTS (PER SERVING)
Calories: 208   Carbohydrates: 26.8 g   Cholesterol: 48 mg
Fat: 1.9 g   Fiber: 0.9 g   Protein: 15.6 g   Sodium: 120 mg

Savory Veal Stew

From start to finish, you can prepare this stew in under an hour.

Yield: *8 servings*

1. Bring 1 cup of water to boil in small saucepan. Stir in the barley, reduce the heat to low, and cook covered for 30 minutes.

2. Coat a large skillet with olive oil cooking spray and place over medium-low heat. Add the veal and sauté until lightly brown on all sides. Drain any fat from the skillet.

3. Add the cooked barley, along with the remaining ingredients. Mix well and increase the heat to medium.

4. Cook covered for 20 minutes, or until the veal is tender.

5. Spoon into bowls and serve.

SLOW-COOKER INSTRUCTIONS

1. Place all of the ingredients in a slow-cooker with just enough water to cover. Mix well.

2. Cook on Setting 3 for 8 to 10 hours.

½ cup barley, rinsed and drained

1 pound veal stew meat, cut into bite-sized cubes and trimmed of excess fat

8 ounces no-sodium tomato sauce

3 cloves garlic, thinly sliced

1 tablespoon paprika

1 teaspoon ground cumin

2 tablespoons chopped fresh basil

NUTRITIONAL FACTS (PER SERVING)

Calories: 115   Carbohydrates: 11.4 g   Cholesterol: 48 mg

Fat: 1.8 g   Fiber 2.3 g   Protein: 13.7 g   Sodium: 55 mg

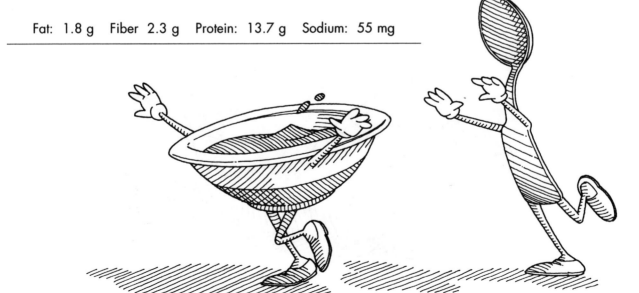

My Mother's Codfish Stew

Yield: *8 servings*

8-ounce can no-sodium tomato sauce

1/2 cup dry white wine

1 1/2 cups water

2 tablespoons fat-free French salad dressing

1 1/2 pounds codfish fillets, cut into 1-inch slices

3 medium potatoes, peeled and cut into bite-sized cubes

3 medium carrots, peeled and cut into 2-inch slices

1 medium onion, thinly sliced

2 tablespoons chopped fresh tarragon

1/4 teaspoon ground black pepper

Low in calories and high in beneficial omega-3 fatty acids, fish is a healthful dietary choice.

1. Combine all of the ingredients in a large pot and mix well.

2. Cook covered over medium heat for 45 minutes, or until the fish is tender.

3. Spoon into bowls and serve.

SLOW-COOKER INSTRUCTIONS

1. Place all of the ingredients in a slow-cooker with just enough water to cover. Mix well.

2. Cook on Setting 2 for 6 to 8 hours.

NUTRITIONAL FACTS (PER SERVING)

Calories: 124   Carbohydrates: 12 g   Cholesterol: 37 mg
Fat: 0.7 g   Fiber: 0.8 g   Protein: 16.8 g   Sodium: 162 mg

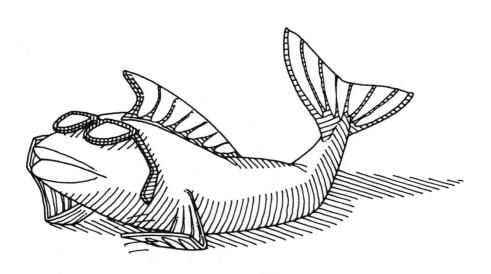

Seafood Gumbo

Okra adds flavor and thickness to this delicious Southern seafood stew. The longer it cooks, the better it tastes, so I usually make this stew in a slow-cooker.

1. Bring 2½ cups of water to boil in a 6-quart pot. Stir in the rice, reduce the heat to low, and cover. Cook for 35 minutes or until the rice is tender and easily fluffs with a fork. Add the tomatoes, okra, and 7½ cups of water to the rice. Simmer covered for 20 minutes.

2. Add all of the remaining ingredients and mix well. Continue to cook uncovered for 45 minutes, or until the fish and okra are tender.

3. Remove the bay leaves before serving.

SLOW-COOKER INSTRUCTIONS

1. Place all of the ingredients in a slow-cooker with just enough water to cover. Mix well.

2. Cook on Setting 2 for 8 to 10 hours.

NUTRITIONAL FACTS (PER SERVING)
Calories: 143   Carbohydrates: 23.7 g   Cholesterol: 0 mg
Fat: 1.1 g   Fiber: 2.9 g   Protein: 10.2 g   Sodium: 236 mg

VARIATION

• To enjoy this gumbo as a soup, add all of the ingredients to the cooked rice, along with 2 additional cups of water. Simmer for 30 minutes or until the fish is cooked and the okra is just tender.

Yield: *10 servings*

1 cup brown rice

28-ounce can no-sodium crushed tomatoes

10 ounces fresh okra, cut into 2-inch pieces*

1 pound flounder, whiting, and/or cod fillets, cut into 1-inch slices

2 large onions, coarsely chopped

2 celery ribs, sliced

1 large green bell pepper, coarsely chopped

¼ cup chopped fresh parsley

¼ cup Worcestershire sauce

1 teaspoon ground cumin

½ teaspoon chopped fresh thyme leaves

½ teaspoon ground white pepper

2 bay leaves

* Can use a 10-ounce box frozen cut okra, thawed.

Seafood Jambalaya

Yield: *8 servings*

1 1/2 cups brown rice

28-ounce can no-sodium crushed tomatoes

1 pound flounder, whiting, and/or cod fillets, cut into 1-inch slices

1 medium celery rib, coarsely chopped

1 medium onion, coarsely chopped

1 garlic clove, finely chopped

2 medium scallions, light green and white part only, chopped

1 bay leaf

1 tablespoon chopped fresh oregano

1 tablespoon chopped fresh basil

1 teaspoon chopped fresh thyme

1/2 teaspoon crushed red pepper flakes, or to taste

1/2 teaspoon ground black pepper

This great Cajun dish calls for your choice of kosher fish fillets.

1. Bring 3 3/4 cups water to boil in a 6-quart pot. Stir in the rice, reduce the heat to low, and cover. Cook for 35 minutes or until the rice is tender and easily fluffs with a fork. Add the crushed tomatoes and 1 1/4 cups of water and simmer for 5 minutes.

2. Add all of the remaining ingredients to the pot and stir well.

3. Cook uncovered over low heat for 45 minutes, or until the fish is tender.

4. Remove the bay leaf before serving.

SLOW-COOKER INSTRUCTIONS

1. Place all of the ingredients in a slow-cooker with just enough water to cover. Mix well.

2. Cook on Setting 2 for 8 to 10 hours.

NUTRITIONAL FACTS (PER SERVING)

Calories: 198   Carbohydrates: 33.7 g   Cholesterol: 0 mg
Fat: 1.6 g   Fiber: 2.5 g   Protein: 12.5 g   Sodium: 120 mg

Old-Time Chulent

A traditional Sabbath stew, chulent is cooked at least halfway before the Sabbath begins; it is then kept warm in a crockpot or slow-cooker, or in a pot on top of a blech. As chulent is heated for a great many hours, its ingredients must be able to stand up to a lengthy cooking time. A mixture of hardy black beans, navy beans, and black-eyed peas are suggested. When using the stovetop to prepare this recipe, use canned beans. Both Kedem and Unger's make canned chulent bean mix.

Yield: *10 servings*

1 pound veal stew meat, cubed and trimmed of excess fat

1 pound veal bones

16-ounce can chulent bean mix*

1/2 cup barley, rinsed and drained

2 tablespoons red wine vinegar

3 medium carrots, peeled and cut into quarters

1 large onion, coarsely chopped

2 garlic cloves, thinly sliced

1 tablespoon paprika

1 teaspoon ground cumin

2 bay leaves

3 small potatoes, scrubbed

4 medium eggs

1. Bring 4 cups of water to boil in a 6-quart pot.

2. While the water is heating up, coat a large skillet with olive oil cooking spray and place over medium-low heat. Add the veal and sauté until lightly brown on all sides. Place the veal on paper towels and pat to absorb any excess oil. Transfer the veal and veal bones to the pot.

3. Add the beans, barley, vinegar, carrots, onion, garlic, paprika, cumin, and bay leaves to the pot and mix well.

4. Place the potatoes and eggs on top of the other ingredients. Reduce the heat to low, cover, and cook for 2 hours.

5. Remove and discard the bay leaves. Shell the eggs and discard the yolks. Chop the egg whites.

6. Ladle the chulent into bowls, garnish with egg whites, and serve.

CROCKPOT INSTRUCTIONS

1. Add all of the ingredients, except the potatoes and eggs, in a 5-quart crockpot and mix well. Place the potatoes and eggs on top of the other ingredients. Add enough water to just cover.

2. Cook on Low setting for 8 to 10 hours.

* If using a crockpot, use 1 cup mixture of dried black beans, navy beans, and black-eyed peas, rinsed and drained, or 1 cup commercial dried chulent bean mixture (navy, kidney, and cranberry beans).

NUTRITIONAL FACTS (PER SERVING)
Calories: 182   Carbohydrates: 27.1 g   Cholesterol 38 mg
Fat: 1.8 g   Fiber: 7.5 g   Protein: 15.9 g   Sodium: 104 mg

Super Sauces

The right sauce can add the perfect touch to a wide variety of dishes. I use the following sauces as flavorful ingredients in a number of stews and entrées. They are also great toppers for many vegetables, beans, and pastas. As the Italian Tomato Sauce and Spicy Tomato Sauce benefit from a lengthy cooking time, crockpot instructions have been included along with the conventional cooking methods.

Spicy Tomato Sauce

Yield: *5 cups*

2 cups water

28-ounce can no-sodium crushed tomatoes

1 cup red and/or green bell peppers chopped

1 large onion, thinly sliced

1 cup Fresh Homemade Salsa (page 34), or a low-sodium commercial variety

1/2 teaspoon crushed red pepper flakes

This zesty tomato sauce will add spark to any dish. Be sure to try it with Mushroom Rice (page 170) or as the sauce in Zesty Chicken (page 111).

1. Bring the water to boil in a 3-quart pot. Add the tomatoes and reduce the heat to low.

2. Add all of the remaining ingredients to the pot and simmer partially covered for 45 minutes, stirring occasionally. (You can continue to simmer the sauce several hours for a richer flavor.)

3. Spoon over hot pasta or steamed fresh vegetables.

4. Stored in a tightly sealed container and refrigerated, this sauce will keep for 2 weeks.

CROCKPOT INSTRUCTIONS

1. Place all of the ingredients in a 3-quart crockpot. Add enough water to just cover.

2. Cook on Low for 6 to 8 hours.

NUTRITIONAL FACTS (PER 1/2-CUP SERVING)

Calories: 29   Carbohydrates: 6.1 g   Cholesterol: 0 mg
Fat: 0.2 g   Fiber: 1.8 g   Protein: 0.9 g   Sodium: 211 mg

Top: Long Beach Stuffed Peppers (page 144)
Left: Seafood Lasagna (page 128)
Right: Old-Time Chulent (page 85)

Top Left: Peanut Butter Chicken (page 98)

Top Right and Bottom Left: Cold Sesame Noodles (page 36)

Bottom Right: Spinach-Mushroom Medley (page 171)

Spicy Barbecue Sauce

This sauce, which makes a great baste for grilled chicken and vegetables, also adds spark to a number of stews and bean dishes. Try it
in Spicy Barbecue Chulent (page 91).

Yield: *2 cups*

1 small onion, cut into
  chunks

1 garlic clove, cut in half

2 tablespoons molasses

2 tablespoons Dijon-style
  mustard

$\frac{1}{4}$ teaspoon paprika

1 cup water

1. Place the onion and garlic in a food processor or blender and
purée for 5 seconds. Add the remaining ingredients and purée another 5 seconds. Slowly stir in up to $\frac{1}{2}$ cup of water to form a thick but
pourable liquid.

2. Use as a baste or add to another recipe.

3. Stored in a tightly sealed container and refrigerated, this sauce
will keep for 2 weeks.

NUTRITIONAL FACTS (PER 2-TABLESPOON SERVING)
Calories: 14   Carbohydrates: 3.1 g   Cholesterol: 0 mg
Fat: 0.1 g   Fiber: 0.2 g   Protein: 0.3 g   Sodium: 79 mg

Italian Tomato Sauce

Yield: *4 cups*

2 cups water

3 cups peeled, chopped ripe tomatoes, or 28-ounce can no-sodium peeled tomatoes

1 medium onion, finely chopped

3 garlic cloves, minced

8 ounces mushrooms, coarsely chopped

1 teaspoon chopped fresh rosemary leaves

1 teaspoon chopped fresh parsley

1/4 teaspoon chopped fresh oregano

1/8 teaspoon ground black pepper

1 bay leaf

The longer this sauce simmers, the richer its flavor will be. Try it on Lima Beans with Tarragon (page 176), or use it instead of commercial tomato sauce in any recipe.

1. Bring the water to boil in a large pot. Add the tomatoes and reduce the heat to low.

2. Add all of the remaining ingredients to the pot and simmer partially covered for 45 minutes, stirring occasionally. (You can continue to simmer the sauce several hours for a richer flavor.)

3. Remove and discard the bay leaf before spooning over hot pasta or steamed fresh vegetables.

4. Stored in a tightly sealed container and refrigerated, this sauce will keep for 2 weeks.

CROCKPOT INSTRUCTIONS

1. Place the tomatoes, onion, garlic, and mushrooms in a 3-quart crockpot.

2. Add 1 tablespoon rosemary, ½ teaspoon oregano, and ½ teaspoon black pepper to the pot and stir well. Add enough water to just cover.

3. Cook on Low setting for 6 to 8 hours.

NUTRITIONAL FACTS (PER ½-CUP SERVING)
Calories: 33   Carbohydrates: 6.8 g   Cholesterol: 0 mg
Fat: 0.4 g   Protein: 1.8 g   Fiber: 2.4 g   Sodium: 85 mg

Chulent Dijonnaise

This is a great vegetarian dish. Texturized vegetable protein may be used in place of the vegetable protein crumbles.

1. Bring 2 cups of water to boil in a large pot. Add the vegetable protein crumbles, reduce the heat to low, and simmer for 5 minutes.

2. Add the remaining ingredients and mix well.

3. Increase the heat to medium, and cook covered for 45 minutes.

4. Spoon over brown rice or noodles.

SLOW-COOKER INSTRUCTIONS

1. Place all of the ingredients in a slow-cooker with just enough water to cover. Mix well.

2. Cook setting 3 for 8 to 10 hours.

Yield: *8 servings*

8 ounces vegetable protein crumbles

16-ounce can cooked red kidney beans, rinsed and drained*

2 large onions, coarsely chopped

2 tablespoons Dijon-style mustard

2 tablespoons honey

* If using a crockpot, use 1 cup dried red kidney beans, rinsed and drained.

NUTRITIONAL FACTS (PER SERVING)

Calories: 145   Carbohydrates: 23.9 g   Cholesterol: 0 mg
Fat: 0.4 g   Fiber: 6.0 g   Protein: 12.2 g   Sodium: 316 mg

Tex-Mex Chulent

Yield: *8 servings*

4 medium potatoes, scrubbed

1 cup barley, rinsed and drained

16-ounce can black beans or pinto beans*

1 cup Fresh Homemade Salsa (page 34), or low-sodium commercial variety

2 drops hot pepper sauce

* If using a crockpot, use 1 cup dried beans, rinsed and drained.

You can use your favorite commercial salsa or make your own to use with this chulent.

1. Bring 4 cups water to a boil in a 6-quart pot.

2. Add the potatoes and boil 5 minutes. Reduce the heat to medium, stir in the barley, and cook covered for 30 minutes.

3. Add the remaining ingredients and cook another 30 minutes, or until the potatoes are soft. Coarsely mash the potatoes.

4. Spoon into bowls and serve.

SLOW-COOKER INSTRUCTIONS

1. Place all of the ingredients in a slow-cooker with just enough water to cover. Mix well.

2. Cook on setting 3 for 8 to 10 hours.

NUTRITIONAL FACTS (PER SERVING)
Calories: 200   Carbohydrates: 40.1 g   Cholesterol: 0 mg
Fat: 1 g   Fiber: 8.4 g   Protein: 9.1 g   Sodium: 42 mg

VARIATION

• Wrap 8 soft flour tortillas in wax paper and microwave for 45 seconds on High. Spoon chulent into each shell, along with shredded lettuce, diced tomatoes, and shredded lowfat or nonfat cheese (for a dairy meal). Fold the tortillas over the filling and enjoy.

Spicy Barbecue Chulent

Spicy barbecue sauce gives this chulent special flavor.

Yield: *8 servings*

1. Bring 2½ cups of water to boil in a small saucepan. Stir in the rice, reduce the heat to low, and cover. Cook for 35 minutes, or until the rice is tender and easily fluffs with a fork.

2. While the rice is cooking, bring 4 cups water to boil in a large pot. Add the remaining ingredients and mix well. Cook covered over medium heat for 30 minutes. Add the cooked rice and stir well.

3. Spoon into bowls and serve.

SLOW-COOKER INSTRUCTIONS

1. Place all of the ingredients in a slow-cooker with just enough water to cover. Mix well.

2. Cook on setting 3 for 8 to 10 hours.

1 cup brown rice

16-ounce can no-sodium crushed tomatoes

16-ounce can red kidney beans*

1 large onion, thinly sliced

2 tablespoons Spicy Barbecue Sauce (page 87), or a low-sodium commercial variety

1 tablespoon Worcestershire sauce

* If using a crockpot, use 1 cup dried kidney beans, rinsed and drained.

NUTRITIONAL FACTS (PER SERVING)

Calories: 183   Carbohydrates: 36.2 g   Cholesterol: 0 mg
Fat: 1.1 g   Fiber: 4.8 g   Protein: 7.7 g   Sodium: 136 mg

Vegetarian Herb Chulent

Yield: *8 servings*

1 cup wild rice

1 cup dry white wine

16-ounce can vegetarian bean
    mix*

1 large onion, coarsely
    chopped

1 garlic clove, finely chopped

1/4 cup chopped fresh parsley

1/4 cup chopped fresh celery

1/4 cup chopped fresh rosemary

1/4 cup chopped fresh tarragon

1 tablespoon ground cumin

2 bay leaves

* If using a crockpot, use 1 cup dried
    bean mixture, rinsed and drained.

Kedem and Unger's both make good-quality canned vegetarian bean mixtures. The Kedem brand includes kidney beans, chick peas, Romano beans, black-eyed peas, black beans, and lima beans. Unger's version includes cranberry beans, red kidney beans, and white beans. Of course, feel free to use your choice of canned bean combinations.

1. Bring 2½ cups of water to a boil in a 6-quart pot. Stir in the rice, reduce the heat to low, and simmer covered for 45 minutes.

2. Add the remaining ingredients to the pot and mix well.

3. Increase the heat to medium and cook covered for 20 minutes, or until the vegetables and rice are tender.

4. Remove the bay leaves before spooning into bowls and serving.

SLOW-COOKER INSTRUCTIONS

1. Place all of the ingredients in a slow-cooker with just enough water to cover. Mix well.

2. Cook on setting 3 for 8 to 10 hours

NUTRITIONAL FACTS (PER SERVING)
Calories: 199   Carbohydrates: 35.5 g   Cholesterol: 0 mg
Fat: 1 g   Fiber: 8.3 g   Protein: 9.8 g   Sodium: 87 mg

Light Beer Chulent

Light beer adds a surprisingly pleasant flavor to this chulent.

Yield: *8 servings*

1. Bring 4 cups of water to boil in a 6-quart pot. Add the barley, reduce the heat to medium, and cook covered for 30 minutes.

2. Add the carrots, bell peppers, tomato sauce, chick peas, and onion to the pot. Pour the beer over the ingredients and mix well.

3. Cook covered for 30 minutes.

4. Spoon into bowls and serve hot.

SLOW-COOKER INSTRUCTIONS

1. Place all of the ingredients in a slow-cooker with just enough water to cover. Mix well.

2. Cook on setting 3 for 8 to 10 hours.

1 cup barley, rinsed and drained

2 medium carrots, peeled and cut into eighths

2 cups red and/or green bell peppers, chopped

8-ounce can no-sodium tomato sauce

16-ounce can chick peas*

1 large onion, thinly sliced

12 ounces light beer

* If using a crockpot, use 1 cup dried chick peas, rinsed and drained.

NUTRITIONAL FACTS (PER SERVING)
Calories: 125   Carbohydrates: 27.9 g   Cholesterol: 0 mg
Fat: 0.6 g   Fiber: 5.7 g   Protein: 4.4 g   Sodium: 130 mg

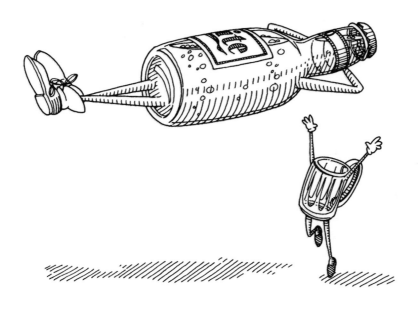

5.

Chicken Dishes

Chicken is a healthy ingredient choice. It is very versatile and lends itself to many different kinds of recipes. I love to try out different ingredient combinations when cooking with chicken. I have created a variety of delicious dishes by combining chicken with different herbs, spices, fruits, vegetables, and grains.

Reputable kosher butchers sell chickens that have been ritually slaughtered, then soaked and salted according to Jewish law. This soaking and salting process leaves kosher chickens with a somewhat higher (but varying) sodium content than non-kosher varieties.

Compared to most other meats, chicken is low in fat and calories. To reduce its fat content even further, it is important to remove the skin and any visible fat before cooking. As the fat content of white meat chicken is much lower than dark meat, my recipes call for skinless chicken breast cutlets only. In addition to being low in fat, chicken cutlets require very little preparation and minimal cooking time. The chicken needs only to be washed and trimmed of excess fat and then baked in a 350°F oven for 20 to 30 minutes.

To reduce the fat content of chicken cutlets even further, you can cook them on a roasting rack that has been set in the bottom of a baking dish. This metal rack allows any remaining fat in the chicken to drip into the bottom of the pan below. Also available are vertical roasting racks for cooking whole chickens. Although all of my chicken recipes call for white meat cutlets, feel free to use other chicken parts or even whole chickens if you prefer. Just be sure to remove the skin and as much visible fat before cooking. When opting to use the whole chicken, I suggest using either a vertical or horizontal roasting rack.

One of the biggest complaints with oven-baked chicken cutlets is that they tend to be dry. The key here is to keep an eye on the cooking time. As soon as the chicken is cooked—when it is no longer pink inside—remove it from the oven. This generally takes between 20 to 30 minutes, depending on the thickness of the cutlet. Overcooking will result in dryness every time. You will find that when properly cooked and served with moist, flavorful sauces and toppings, baked chicken breast cutlets are delicious.

Orange Chicken

Yield: *8 servings*

An old family favorite that never fails to please.

1 cup brown rice

2 pounds chicken breast cutlets, rinsed and patted dry

4 drops hot pepper sauce

1 tablespoon cinnamon

1 cup orange juice

1 small bunch broccoli, cut into thin strips

1 medium orange, peeled and sliced, or 8-ounce can Mandarin orange slices

1. Bring 2½ cups of water to boil in a small saucepan. Stir in the rice, reduce the heat to low, and cover. Cook for 35 minutes, or until the rice is tender and easily fluffs with a fork.

2. Preheat the oven to 350°F. Coat a 9-x-13-inch baking dish with olive oil cooking spray and set aside.

3. Add the pepper sauce to the cooked rice and mix well. Spread the rice evenly on the bottom of the baking dish

4. Place the chicken cutlets on top of the rice and sprinkle with cinnamon. Spoon the orange juice over the chicken.

5. Bake for 20 minutes, then top the cutlets with broccoli strips and orange slices. Continue to bake another 10 minutes, or until the chicken is no longer pink inside.

6. Spoon the rice onto individual plates. Cut the chicken into wedges and arrange on top of the rice. Serve topped with orange slices and broccoli strips.

NUTRITIONAL FACTS (PER SERVING)
Calories: 240   Carbohydrates: 24 g   Cholesterol: 66 mg
Fat: 2.6 g   Fiber: 1 g   Protein: 28.8 g   Sodium: 82 mg

VARIATIONS

• Instead of broccoli, try using other vegetables to top the chicken. Good choices include asparagus, cauliflower, and Brussels sprouts.

• To reduce the cooking time, use instant rice instead of the longer-cooking variety.

Honey-Mustard Chicken

A simple dish with a sweet, tangy flavor.

Yield: *8 servings*

1. Preheat the oven to 350°F. Coat a 9-x-13-inch baking dish with olive oil cooking spray. Place the chicken cutlets in the baking dish and set aside.

2. Combine the honey, mustard, and water in a small bowl. Brush this mixture over the chicken.

3. Bake for 20 to 30 minutes, or until the chicken is no longer pink inside.

4. Serve hot alongside your favorite vegetable side dish. Try it with Baked Butternut Squash (page 155).

2 pounds chicken breast cutlets, rinsed and patted dry

3 tablespoons honey

2 tablespoons Dijon-style mustard

¼ cup water

NUTRITIONAL FACTS (PER SERVING)
Calories: 156 Carbohydrates: 6.8 g Cholesterol: 66 mg
Fat: 2 g Fiber 0.1 g Protein: 26.5 g Sodium: 125 mg

Peanut Butter Chicken

Yield: *8 servings*

2 pounds chicken breast cutlets, rinsed and patted dry

1 tablespoon reduced-fat creamy peanut butter

1 teaspoon low-sodium soy sauce

$1/4$ cup water

1 teaspoon sesame seeds

The kids will love this one.

1. Preheat the oven to 350°F. Coat a 9-x-13-inch baking dish with olive oil cooking spray.

2. Place the chicken cutlets in the bottom of the baking dish and set aside.

3. Combine the peanut butter, soy sauce, and water in a microwave-safe bowl. Microwave for 30 seconds on High, or heat the ingredients in a small saucepan over medium-low heat. Stir until smooth and well-mixed. Spoon this mixture over the chicken, then sprinkle with sesame seeds.

4. Bake for 20 to 30 minutes, or until the chicken is no longer pink inside.

5. Serve hot over brown rice or alongside Cold Sesame Noodles (page 36).

NUTRITIONAL FACTS (PER SERVING)
Calories: 144   Carbohydrates: 0.1 g   Cholesterol: 66 mg
Fat: 2.8 g   Fiber: 0.1 g   Protein: 27 g   Sodium: 110 mg

Quick Mexican Chicken

You'll love this spicy, flavorful chicken dish.

Yield: *8 servings*

1. Preheat the oven to 350°F. Coat a 9-x-13-inch baking dish with olive oil cooking spray.

2. Combine the Mexican seasoning, pepper sauce, and water in a small bowl. Rub this mixture into the chicken cutlets, then place them in the baking dish.

3. Bake for 20 to 30 minutes, or until the chicken is no longer pink inside.

4. Serve with brown rice and a cool, crisp green salad.

2 pounds chicken breast cutlets, rinsed and patted dry

2 tablespoons dried Mexican seasoning, or 1 tablespoon chili powder

2 drops hot pepper sauce

2 tablespoons water

NUTRITIONAL FACTS (PER SERVING)
Calories: 135   Carbohydrates: 1 g   Cholesterol: 66 mg
Fat: 2.2 g   Fiber: 0.6 g   Protein: 26.6 g   Sodium: 96 mg

VARIATION

• For a real Mexican fiesta, serve the chicken topped with shredded lettuce, diced tomatoes, and crushed baked tortilla chips (unsalted).

Parsley, Sage, Rosemary, & Thyme Chicken

Yield: *8 servings*

2 pounds chicken breast cutlets, rinsed and patted dry

¼ cup chopped fresh parsley

¼ cup fresh whole-leaf sage

¼ cup fresh rosemary

¼ cup fresh thyme

¼ cup water

Are you going to Scarborough Fair? This dish is tasty whether you use fresh herbs or dried.

1. Preheat the oven to 350°F. Coat a 9-x-13-inch baking dish with olive oil cooking spray.

2. Combine the parsley, sage, rosemary, thyme, and water in a small bowl. Rub this mixture into the chicken cutlets, then place in the baking dish.

3. Bake for 20 to 30 minutes, or until the chicken is no longer pink inside.

4. Serve over angel hair pasta.

NUTRITIONAL FACTS (PER SERVING)

Calories: 138   Carbohydrates: 11.9 g   Cholesterol: 66 mg

Fat: 2.2 g   Fiber: 0.3 g   Protein: 26.6 g   Sodium: 80 mg

Fresh Herbs or Dried?

Flavorful herbs and spices are important for transforming many bland low-fat and sodium-free dishes into tasty, mouthwatering delights. Unless otherwise specified, the herbs called for in my recipes are fresh, but when dried varieties are all that are available, use the following equivalency formula:

1 tablespoon fresh herbs = 1 teaspoon dried

Sweet Chicken with Vegetables

A main course and salad all in one.

Yield: *8 servings*

1. Preheat the oven to 350°F. Coat a 9-x-13-inch baking dish with olive oil cooking spray.

2. Place the chicken cutlets in the baking dish and set aside.

3. Combine the honey, mustard, and water in a small bowl. Spoon this mixture over the chicken.

4. Bake for 15 minutes, then top the cutlets with cucumber slices and tomatoes. Continue to bake another 5 to 10 minutes, or until the chicken is no longer pink inside.

5. Transfer to a serving platter and enjoy hot.

2 pounds chicken breast cutlets, rinsed and patted dry

1/4 cup honey

2 tablespoons Dijon-style mustard

1/2 cup water

2 medium-sized cucumbers, unpeeled and cut into 2-inch slices

1 cup ripe cherry tomatoes, halved

NUTRITIONAL FACTS (PER SERVING)

Calories: 178   Carbohydrates: 11.9 g   Cholesterol: 66 mg
Fat: 2.2 g   Fiber: 0.9 g   Protein: 27.2 g   Sodium: 128 mg

VARIATION

- Instead of the honey-mustard mixture, use 1/4 cup fat-free Honey-Dijon salad dressing.

Salsa Chicken

Yield: *8 servings*

2 pounds chicken breast cutlets, rinsed and patted dry

1 cup no-sodium crushed tomatoes, or chopped fresh tomatoes

1/2 small onion, coarsely chopped

1/2 small green bell pepper, coarsely chopped

1 small jalapeño pepper, seeded and finely chopped

1 small green chile pepper, seeded and finely chopped

2 medium carrots, peeled and coarsely chopped

1 garlic clove, sliced

1 cup dry white wine

Before serving this Southwestern-style chicken dish, top the cutlets with a few crushed, baked tortilla chips (unsalted).

1. Preheat the oven to 350°F. Coat a 9-x-13-inch baking dish with olive oil cooking spray.

2. Place the chicken cutlets in the baking dish and set aside.

3. Combine the tomatoes, onion, bell pepper, jalapeño and green chile peppers, carrots, garlic, and wine in a small bowl. Spoon this mixture over the cutlets.

4. Bake for 20 to 30 minutes, or until the chicken is no longer pink inside.

5. Serve hot.

NUTRITIONAL FACTS (PER SERVING)

Calories: 170   Carbohydrates: 4.8 g   Cholesterol: 66 mg
Fat: 2 g   Fiber: 1.4 g   Protein: 27.1 g   Sodium: 124 mg

VARIATION

• Cut the cooked chicken into bite-sized pieces and spoon into warmed taco shells. Top with shredded lettuce.

Thirty-Second Salsa Chicken

When you don't have the time to peel and chop . . .

Yield: *8 servings*

1. Preheat the oven to 350°F. Coat a 9-x-13-inch baking dish with olive oil cooking spray.

2. Place the chicken cutlets in the baking dish and cover with salsa.

3. Bake for 20 to 30 minutes, or until the chicken is no longer pink inside.

4. Top with crushed baked tortilla chips, if desired.

2 pounds chicken breast cutlets, rinsed and patted dry

12-ounce jar commercial salsa (mild, medium, or hot)

NUTRITIONAL FACTS (PER SERVING)

Calories: 144   Carbohydrates: 1.4 g   Cholesterol: 66 mg
Fat: 1.9 g   Fiber: 0.3 g   Protein: 26.3 g   Sodium: 276 mg

VARIATIONS

- Cut the cooked chicken into bite-sized pieces and spoon into warmed taco shells. Top with shredded lettuce and extra salsa.

- If you have any Fresh Homemade Salsa (page 34) on hand, be sure to use it instead of the commercial variety.

Chicken with Potatoes Lyonnaise

Yield: *8 servings*

2 pounds chicken breast cutlets, rinsed and patted dry

8 medium potatoes, peeled and thinly sliced

2 medium Vidalia or other sweet onion, thinly sliced

¼ cup dry white wine

¼ cup chopped fresh parsley

2 tablespoons fresh thyme

¼ teaspoon ground black pepper

This dish is so quick and easy, I made it often while I was in medical school.

1. Preheat the oven to 350°F. Coat a 9-x-13-inch baking dish with olive oil cooking spray.

2. Arrange the potato slices in an even layer in the bottom of the baking dish. Place the onion slices on top of the potatoes.

3. Combine the wine, parsley, thyme, and black pepper in a small bowl. Using a pastry brush, coat the potatoes and onions with a quarter of this herb mixture.

4. Place the chicken cutlets on top of the potato and onion slices, and coat them with half of the herb mixture.

5. Place in the oven. As the chicken bakes, baste it with the remaining herb mixture. Bake for 20 to 30 minutes, or until the chicken is no longer pink inside.

6. Cut the chicken into wedge-shaped pieces. Arrange the potatoes and onion slices on individual plates and top with the chicken wedges.

NUTRITIONAL FACTS (PER SERVING)

Calories: 215   Carbohydrates: 18.6 g   Cholesterol: 66 mg
Fat: 2.1 g   Fiber: 2.4 g   Protein: 28.9 g   Sodium: 90 mg

Arroz con Pollo

This Spanish dish of "chicken with rice," is a hearty, flavorful one-pot meal that cooks in less than 45 minutes.

1. Bring the stock to boil in a large saucepan.

2. Stir in the rice, bell peppers, onion, garlic, and turmeric, and return to a boil. Add the chicken, reduce the heat to low, and simmer covered for 20 to 30 minutes.

3. Add the peas and simmer covered another 10 minutes, or until the rice is tender.

4. Transfer to a serving bowl and enjoy immediately.

NUTRITIONAL FACTS (PER SERVING)
Calories: 238   Carbohydrates: 22.5 g   Cholesterol: 66 mg
Fat: 2.7 g   Fiber: 1.4 g   Protein: 29.4 g   Sodium: 150 mg

Yield: *8 servings*

2 pounds chicken breast cutlets, rinsed, patted dry, and cut into bite-sized pieces

2 cups homemade Chicken Stock (page 39), or water

1 cup brown rice

1 cup sliced red and green bell peppers

1 large onion, coarsely chopped

2 garlic cloves, thinly sliced

1 teaspoon ground turmeric

1 cup fresh or frozen peas

Marjoram-Thyme Chicken

Yield: *8 servings*

2 pounds chicken breast cutlets, rinsed and patted dry

¼ cup chopped fresh parsley

¼ cup fresh ground marjoram

¼ cup fresh thyme leaves

1 cup dry white wine

½ cup carrot slices

Brushed with a deep green blend of marjoram and thyme, these chicken cutlets look especially appealing when topped with bright orange carrot slices.

1. Preheat the oven to 350°F. Coat a 9-x-13-inch baking dish with olive oil cooking spray. Place the chicken cutlets in the baking dish and set aside.

2. Combine the parsley, marjoram, thyme, and wine in a small saucepan. Boil uncovered for 3 minutes, then remove from the heat. Using a pastry brush, brush this mixture over the chicken.

3. Bake for 20 to 30 minutes, or until chicken is no longer pink inside.

4. Garnish with carrot slices and serve.

NUTRITIONAL FACTS (PER SERVING)

Calories: 164   Carbohydrates: 3.6 g   Cholesterol: 66 mg
Fat: 2.1 g   Fiber: 1 g   Protein: 26.9 g   Sodium: 86 mg

Peachy Chicken

The sweetness of the peaches is complemented by the nutty flavor of the wild rice in this chicken dish.

1. Preheat the oven to 350°F. Coat a 9-x-13-inch baking dish with olive oil cooking spray.

2. Bring the water to boil in a small saucepan. Stir in the rice, reduce the heat to low, and cover. Cook for 45 minutes, or until the rice is tender and easily fluffs with a fork.

3. Place the chicken cutlets in the baking dish. Sprinkle with cinnamon and allspice, then cover with the cooked rice.

4. Combine the peaches (and juice), wine, lemon juice, and cloves in a small bowl. Spoon this mixture over the chicken and rice.

5. Bake for 30 to 40 minutes, or until chicken is no longer pink inside.

6. Arrange on a platter and serve.

Yield: *8 servings*

1 $1/4$ cups water

$1/2$ cup wild rice

2 pounds chicken breast cutlets, rinsed and patted dry

1 teaspoon ground cinnamon

$1/2$ teaspoon ground allspice

12-ounce can sliced peaches in pear juice

$1/2$ cup dry white wine

$1/2$ teaspoon lemon juice

2 cloves

NUTRITIONAL FACTS (PER SERVING)

Calories: 200   Carbohydrates: 13.9 g   Cholesterol: 66 mg
Fat: 2.3 g   Fiber: 1.8 g   Protein: 13.9 g   Sodium: 84 mg

Time-Saving Tip

When time is of the essence and the dish you're preparing calls for rice, substitute instant rice for the longer-cooking variety. This will cut the cooking time substantially.

Garlic Chicken

Yield: *8 servings*

2 pounds chicken breast cutlets, rinsed and patted dry

2 tablespoons garlic powder

1 tablespoon paprika

Cloves from 1 head of garlic, peeled and left whole

1 cup dry white wine

1/4 cup chopped fresh parsley

1 tablespoon chopped fresh basil

1/4 teaspoon ground black pepper

Whenever I make this dish, the wonderful aromatic smell of garlic fills the air and stimulates the appetite.

1. Preheat the oven to 350°F. Coat a 9-x-13-inch baking dish with olive oil cooking spray.

2. Place the chicken cutlets in the bottom of the baking dish. Sprinkle with garlic powder and paprika, and arrange the garlic cloves on top. Set aside.

3. Combine the wine, parsley, basil, and black pepper in a small bowl. Spoon this mixture over the chicken.

4. Cover and bake for 15 minutes. Uncover and bake another 5 to 10 minutes, or until the chicken is no longer pink inside.

5. Arrange on a platter and serve alongside brown rice and a fresh vegetable.

NUTRITIONAL FACTS (PER SERVING)
Calories: 161   Carbohydrates: 2.9 g   Cholesterol: 66 mg
Fat: 2 g   Fiber: 0.3 g   Protein: 27 g   Sodium: 81 mg

VARIATION

• Cut the cooked chicken and add it to 8 ounces of cooked pasta. Add the garlic mixture and toss to coat.

Very Cranberry Chicken

A delicious entrée. Enjoy it with a bowl of Autumn Sweet Potato Soup (page 48).

Yield: *8 servings*

1. Preheat the oven to 350°F. Coat a 9-x-13-inch baking dish with olive oil cooking spray.

2. Bring 2½ cups of water to boil in a small saucepan. Stir in the rice, reduce the heat to low, and cover. Cook for 35 minutes, or until the rice is tender and easily fluffs with a fork. Add the cranberry sauce and mix well.

3. Place the chicken cutlets in the baking dish and cover with cranberry-rice mixture.

4. Combine the orange juice, cinnamon, and nutmeg in a small bowl. Spoon this mixture over the chicken and rice.

5. Bake for 30 to 40 minutes, or until the chicken is no longer pink inside.

6. Spoon on a platter and serve.

1 cup brown rice

1 cup Homemade Cranberry Sauce (page 167), or 8-ounce can commercial variety

2 pounds chicken breast cutlets, rinsed and patted dry

1 cup orange juice

½ teaspoon ground cinnamon

¼ teaspoon ground nutmeg

NUTRITIONAL FACTS (PER SERVING)

Calories: 273   Carbohydrates: 32.5 g   Cholesterol: 66 mg
Fat: 2.6 g   Fiber: 0.4 g   Protein: 28.4 g   Sodium: 87 mg

Steamed Hawaiian Chicken

Yield: *8 servings*

2 pounds chicken breast cutlets, rinsed, patted dry, and cut into bite-sized chunks

16-ounce can crushed pineapple in juice

½ cup whole pitted prunes

1½ teaspoons low-sodium soy sauce

1 teaspoon ground ginger

This is a delicious, healthy version of traditional Hawaiian chicken, which is usually breaded and fried.

1. Place an inch of water in the bottom of a microwave-safe steamer. Set the steamer rack inside and add the chicken pieces. Set aside.

2. Combine the pineapple (and juice), prunes, soy sauce, and ginger in a small bowl. Spoon this mixture over the chicken.

3. Cover the steamer and microwave for 15 minutes on High, or until chicken is no longer pink inside.

4. Transfer the chicken to a platter, spoon the sauce on top, and serve.

NUTRITIONAL FACTS (PER SERVING)

Calories: 188   Carbohydrates: 15.1 g   Cholesterol: 66 mg
Fat: 2 g   Fiber: 1.1 g   Protein: 27 g   Sodium: 189 mg

VARIATION

• You can poach the chicken instead of using the microwave for this dish. Place the chicken in a poaching dish and set in the bottom of a pot. Add enough water to just cover. Cover the pot and cook over medium heat for 10 minutes or until the chicken is no longer pink. In a small saucepan, combine the remaining ingredients, and cook over low heat for 5 minutes, stirring frequently. Pour over the chicken.

Center: Chicken Fajitas (page 122) with
Fresh Homemade Salsa (page 34)
Left: Chili con Carne (page 74)
Bottom: Black Bean Soup (page 57)

Left: Grandma Bertha's Split Pea Soup
(page 56)

Top Right: Jack's Carrot Kugel (page 160)

Bottom Right: My Mother's Baked Codfish
(page 131)

Zesty Chicken

This chicken is great served over pasta.

Yield: *8 servings*

1. Preheat the oven to 350°F. Coat a 9-x-13-inch baking dish with olive oil cooking spray. Place the chicken cutlets in the baking dish and set aside.

2. Combine the tomato sauce, carrots, pepper sauce, red pepper flakes, and black pepper in a small bowl. Spoon this mixture over the chicken, and top with the tortilla chips.

3. Bake for 20 to 30 minutes, or until the chicken is no longer pink inside.

4. Serve hot.

2 pounds chicken breast cutlets, rinsed and patted dry

2 cups no-sodium tomato sauce

1 cup coarsely chopped carrots

4 drops hot pepper sauce

1/4 teaspoon crushed red pepper flakes

1/4 teaspoon ground black pepper

2 tablespoons crushed, baked tortilla chips (unsalted)

NUTRITIONAL FACTS (PER SERVING)

Calories: 164 g   Carbohydrates: 7 g   Cholesterol: 66 mg
Fat: 2 g   Fiber: 0.6 g   Protein: 27.7 g   Sodium: 94 mg

Curried Chicken

Yield: *8 servings*

2 pounds chicken breast cutlets, rinsed and patted dry

1 tablespoon ground turmeric

1 tablespoon ground cumin

1 tablespoon garlic powder

1 tablespoon coriander seeds

1 tablespoon cardamom pods

1 tablespoon black peppercorns

1 teaspoon cloves

Exotic aroma and deep flavor make this mildly spicy dish a dinner-time sensation. It is perfect with fragrant basmati rice.

1. Preheat the oven to 350°F. Coat a 9-x-13-inch baking dish with olive oil cooking spray.

2. Place the chicken cutlets in the baking dish and sprinkle with turmeric, cumin, and garlic powder. Set aside.

3. Combine the coriander seeds, cardamom pods, peppercorns, and cloves in a small bowl. Sprinkle this mixture over the chicken.

4. Bake for 20 to 30 minutes, or until the chicken is no longer pink inside.

5. Remove and discard the coriander seeds, cardamom pods, and cloves before serving.

NUTRITIONAL FACTS (PER SERVING)
Calories: 139   Carbohydrates: 1.6 g   Cholesterol: 66 mg
Fat: 2.1 g   Fiber: 0.3 g   Protein: 26.7 g   Sodium: 79 mg

Instant Curried Chicken

Recipes don't come much easier than this one.

1. Preheat the oven to 350°F. Coat a 9-x-13-inch baking dish with olive oil cooking spray.

2. Place the chicken cutlets in the baking dish. Sprinkle with the curry powder and garlic powder.

3. Bake for 20 to 30 minutes, or until chicken is no longer pink inside.

4. Serve hot over basmati rice.

Yield: *8 servings*

2 pounds chicken breast cutlets, rinsed and patted dry

2 tablespoons curry powder

1 teaspoon garlic powder

NUTRITIONAL FACTS (PER SERVING)
Calories: 136   Carbohydrates: 1.2 g   Cholesterol: 66 mg
Fat: 2.1 g   Fiber: 0.5 g   Protein: 26.6 g   Sodium: 78 mg

Chicken Tofu Bake

Yield: *8 servings*

1¾ pounds chicken breast cutlets, rinsed and patted dry

4 ounces firm tofu, patted dry and cut into 1-inch cubes

28-ounce can no-sodium crushed tomatoes

8 ounces mushrooms, sliced

1 medium Vidalia or other sweet onion, thinly sliced

In addition to containing all eight essential amino acids, tofu is high in both protein and calcium. It contains zero cholesterol and very little fat. Packaged tofu with kosher certification is available in many supermarkets.

1. Preheat the oven to 350°F. Coat a 9-x-13-inch baking dish with olive oil cooking spray.

2. Place the chicken cutlets in the baking dish, top with the tofu, and set aside.

3. Combine the crushed tomatoes, mushrooms, and onion slices in a small bowl. Spoon this mixture over the chicken and tofu.

4. Bake for 20 to 30 minutes, or until chicken is no longer pink inside.

5. Transfer to a platter and serve.

NUTRITIONAL FACTS (PER SERVING)
Calories: 156   Carbohydrates: 7.1 g   Cholesterol: 58 mg
Fat: 2.7 g   Fiber: 2.8 g   Protein: 26 g   Sodium: 85 mg

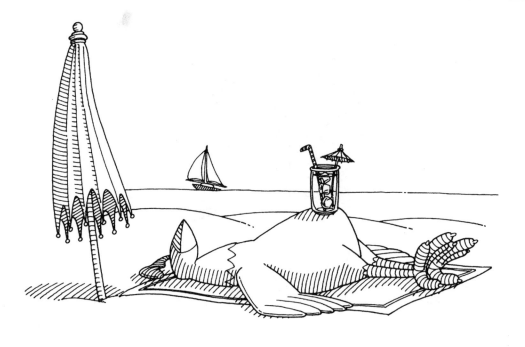

Recipes for Leftover Soup Chicken

In most of the chicken-based soups in Chapter 3, the boiled chicken is removed before the soup is eaten. This may leave you wondering what to do with this leftover chicken, which, although somewhat tasteless, is very low in fat and calories and high in protein. I have found that with the right blend of tasteful ingredients, this otherwise bland chicken can be transformed into dishes that are both delectable and nutritious.

I have created the following recipes specifically for leftover soup chicken. Once skinned, cooked, and deboned, the 2 pounds of chicken called for in the soups, yields about 1 1/2 pounds. You will find the following dishes healthful, easy to make, and tasty enough to serve guests.

Sweet Chicken Salad

Most brands of sweet-and-sour sauce are fat-free and contain only 20 calories per tablespoon.

Yield: *6 servings*

1/2 cup brown rice

1/2 cup raisins

1 1/2 pounds skinless, boneless boiled soup chicken

2 tablespoons sweet-and-sour sauce, or Chinese duck sauce

1 medium Vidalia or other sweet onion, thinly sliced

4 1/2 cups shredded lettuce

1. Bring 2 1/2 cups of water to boil in a small saucepan. Stir in the rice, reduce the heat to low, and cover. Cook for 35 minutes, or until the rice is tender and easily fluffs with a fork.

2. While the rice is cooking, soak the raisins in a cup of warm water for 20 to 30 minutes.

3. Dice the chicken and place it in a microwave-safe bowl along with the sweet-and-sour sauce. Mix well, cover with wax paper, and microwave for 2 minutes on High, or warm in a saucepan over medium-low heat. Add the rice, raisins, and onion. Mix together well.

4. Place the shredded lettuce on a serving platter or individual plates, and spoon the hot chicken mixture on top.

NUTRITIONAL FACTS (PER SERVING)
Calories: 201   Carbohydrates: 26.3 g   Cholesterol: 44 mg
Fat: 1.9 g   Fiber: 1.9 g   Protein: 20.1 g   Sodium: 77 mg

VARIATION

• To reduce the cooking time, use instant rice instead of the longer-cooking variety.

Spanish-Style Chicken with Rice

Yield: *8 servings*

A flavorful, hearty one-dish meal.

1 cup brown rice

2 cups homemade Chicken Stock (page 39), or fat-free commercial variety

1¹/2 pounds skinless, boneless boiled soup chicken

1 cup sliced green and red bell peppers

1 cup fresh or frozen peas

1 large onion, coarsely chopped

2 cloves garlic, thinly sliced

¹/2 teaspoon ground turmeric

¹/2 teaspoon crushed red pepper flakes

1. Bring 2¹/2 cups of water to boil in a small saucepan. Stir in the rice, and reduce the heat to low. Cook covered for 35 minutes, or until the rice is tender and easily fluffs with a fork.

2. Bring the chicken stock to boil in a large skillet. Dice the chicken and add to the skillet along with the bell peppers, peas, onion, garlic, and rice. Stir and return to a boil.

3. Stir in the turmeric and red pepper flakes, reduce the heat to low, and simmer covered for 10 minutes.

4. Serve hot.

NUTRITIONAL FACTS (PER SERVING)

Calories: 133   Carbohydrates: 13.4 g   Cholesterol: 33 mg
Fat: 1.4 g   Fiber: 1.4 g   Protein: 15.3 g   Sodium: 112 mg

VARIATION

• To reduce the cooking time, use instant rice instead of the longer-cooking variety.

Karen's Couscous Chicken

A pasta of North African origin, couscous is made of crushed and steamed semolina. It takes minutes to prepare.

1. Dice the chicken and set aside.

2. Bring the stock to a boil in a large saucepan. Add the chicken along with the carrots, yam, potato, zucchini, and yellow squash. Reduce the heat to low, and simmer partially covered for 10 minutes, or until the vegetables are tender but not mushy.

3. Using a slotted spoon, transfer the chicken and vegetables to a bowl and keep covered.

4. Stir the couscous into the stock and remove the pan from the heat. Cover and let sit for 5 to 10 minutes, or until the couscous fluffs with a fork.

5. Place the couscous on a serving platter, top with the chicken and vegetables, and serve.

Yield: *8 servings*

1 1/2 pounds skinless, boneless boiled soup chicken

2 1/2 cups homemade Chicken Stock (page 39), or fat-free commercial variety

2 medium carrots, peeled and cut into 1-inch slices

1 large yam, peeled and cut into 2-inch slices

1 medium potato, peeled and cut into 2-inch slices

1 medium zucchini, cut into 1/2-inch slices

1 medium yellow squash, cut into 1/2-inch slices

1 cup couscous

NUTRITIONAL FACTS (PER SERVING)

Calories: 195   Carbohydrates: 27.1 g   Cholesterol: 33 mg
Fat: 1.2 g   Fiber: 3 g   Protein: 17.1 g   Sodium: 54 mg

VARIATION

• To reduce the cooking time, use frozen, thawed vegetables instead of fresh.

Waldorf Salad

Yield: *6 servings*

1 1/2 pounds skinless, boneless boiled soup chicken

2 celery ribs, coarsely chopped

1/4 cup chopped walnuts

1 medium apple, peeled and chopped

2 tablespoons fat-free mayonnaise

4 1/2 cups shredded lettuce

Waldorf salad is a great lunch choice on a hot summer day. It is also delicious when made with leftover roasted chicken or turkey.

1. Dice the chicken and place it in a bowl. Add the celery, walnuts, apple, and mayonnaise. Combine well.

2. Cover and refrigerate until chilled.

3. Place the shredded lettuce in a salad bowl or on individual plates. Top with the chicken salad.

NUTRITIONAL FACTS (PER SERVING)
Calories: 119   Carbohydrates: 6 g   Cholesterol: 44 mg
Fat: 2.2 g   Fiber: 1.6 g   Protein: 18.5 g   Sodium: 107 mg

VARIATION

- For added texture and flavor, add 1/4 cup raisins to this salad.

Lunchtime Chicken Salad

Yield: *6 servings*

1 1/2 pounds skinless, boneless boiled soup chicken

2 tablespoons fat-free mayonnaise

2 ribs celery, finely chopped

4 1/2 cups shredded lettuce

This salad takes just minutes to prepare.

1. Dice the chicken and place in a bowl. Add the celery and mayonnaise, and mix well.

2. Cover and refrigerate until chilled.

3. Place the shredded lettuce in a salad bowl or on individual plates. Top with the chicken salad.

NUTRITIONAL FACTS (PER SERVING)
Calories: 99   Carbohydrates: 2.6 g   Cholesterol: 44 mg
Fat: 1.4 g   Fiber: 1 g   Protein: 18.2 g   Sodium: 107 mg

Tropical Chicken Salad

One taste of this salad will transport you to the sunny Caribbean.

1. Dice the chicken and place in a bowl along with the papaya, banana, and onion.

2. Combine the dressing ingredients in a large bowl. Stir well.

3. Pour the dressing over the chicken mixture. Mix well, cover, and refrigerate until chilled.

4. Place the shredded lettuce in a salad bowl or on individual plates. Top with the chilled chicken salad.

NUTRITIONAL FACTS (PER SERVING)

Calories: 132   Carbohydrates: 11 g   Cholesterol: 44 mg
Fat: 1.5 g   Fiber: 2.3 g   Protein: 18.9 g   Sodium: 88 mg

Yield: *6 servings*

1 1/2 pounds skinless, boneless boiled soup chicken

1 large ripe papaya, peeled and cut into 1-inch cubes

1 medium ripe banana, cut into 1-inch slices

1 medium Vidalia or other sweet onion, thinly sliced

4 1/2 cups shredded lettuce

DRESSING

1/4 cup boiling water

1 tablespoon granulated brown sugar

1 teaspoon low-sodium soy sauce

1/2 teaspoon lemon juice

The Well-Dressed Chicken

Yield: *6 servings*

1½ cups golden raisins

1½ pounds skinless, boneless boiled soup chicken

¼ cup fat-free, nondairy salad dressing (your choice)

8 ounces fresh spinach, washed and patted dry

3 tablespoons chopped walnuts

A great dish to include in a buffet-style meal.

1. Soak the raisins in a cup of warm water for 20 to 30 minutes. Drain.

2. Dice the chicken and place in a bowl. Add the salad dressing and mix well.

3. Refrigerate until chilled.

4. Place the spinach in a salad bowl or on individual plates, then top with the chicken salad. Sprinkle with walnuts and raisins.

NUTRITIONAL FACTS (PER SERVING)

Calories: 138   Carbohydrates: 11.3 g   Cholesterol: 44 mg
Fat: 1.9 g   Fiber: 1.3 g   Protein: 19 g   Sodium: 171 mg

Saucy Chicken

Make your own spicy barbecue sauce or use your favorite commercial variety with this recipe.

1. Dice the chicken and place it in a microwave-safe bowl. Add the kidney beans, green beans, and barbecue sauce, and mix well. Cover with wax paper and microwave for 2 minutes on High, or until the green beans are just tender. Or heat the ingredients in a covered saucepan over medium-low heat.

2. Add the onion, corn, and spinach, and mix well.

3. Serve hot.

NUTRITIONAL FACTS (PER SERVING)

Calories: 147   Carbohydrates: 15.6 g   Cholesterol: 33 mg
Fat: 1.4 g   Fiber: 5 g   Protein: 18.5 g   Sodium: 91 mg

VARIATION

- Substitute the kidney beans with other bean varieties, such as black beans, pinto beans, and black-eyed peas.

Yield: *8 servings*

$1 \frac{1}{2}$ pounds skinless, boneless boiled soup chicken

2 cups cooked red kidney beans

1 cup green beans, cut into small pieces

2 tablespoons Spicy Barbecue Sauce (page 87), or commercial variety

1 medium Vidalia or other sweet onion, thinly sliced

$\frac{1}{2}$ cup corn kernels

8 ounces fresh spinach, washed and patted dry

Chicken Fajitas

Yield: *6 fajitas*

1 1/2 pounds skinless, boneless boiled soup chicken

6 soft fat-free flour tortillas (8-inch)

2 tablespoons fajita sauce

2 cups cooked black beans

1 medium Vidalia or other sweet onion, finely chopped

1/4 teaspoon ground black pepper

Feel free to substitute Spicy Barbecue Sauce (page 87) for the fajita sauce in this recipe. For fajitas with a fiery zing, add 1/4 teaspoon chili powder to the filling.

1. Dice the chicken and place it in a large bowl.

2. In a separate bowl, combine the beans, onion, fajita sauce, and black pepper. Add this to the chicken and mix well.

3. Place about 2 tablespoons of the chicken mixture along the center of each tortilla. Fold the sides over the filling. (*See* Forming a Fajita below.) Place the tortillas folded-side down in a microwave-safe baking dish.

4. Cover with wax paper and microwave for 5 minutes on High, or until the filling is hot. Or bake in a 350°F oven about 10 minutes.

5. Serve alongside a cool, crisp green salad.

NUTRITIONAL FACTS (PER SERVING)
Calories: 234   Carbohydrates: 29.1 g   Cholesterol: 44 mg
Fat: 1.7 g   Fiber: 11.7 g   Protein: 25.2 g   Sodium: 278 mg

---

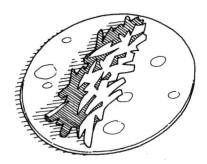

1. Place filling along the center of the tortilla shell.

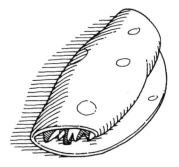

2. Fold the sides over the filling.

Forming a Fajita

Mango Chicken Salad

Mouthwatering ripe mango makes this salad a summer delight.

Yield: *6 servings*

1. Dice the chicken and place it in a large bowl. Add the remaining ingredients and mix well.

2. Cover and refrigerate.

3. Serve chilled.

NUTRITIONAL FACTS (PER SERVING)
Calories: 127   Carbohydrates: 9.1 g   Cholesterol: 44 mg
Fat: 1.6 g   Fiber: 2.4 g   Protein: 19.7 g   Sodium: 79 mg

---

1 1/2 pounds skinless, boneless boiled soup chicken

8 ounces fresh spinach leaves, washed and patted dry

1 large ripe mango, peeled, pitted, and cut into 1-inch cubes

1 large Vidalia or other sweet onion, thinly sliced

1 medium green bell pepper, seeded and thinly sliced

8 ounces fresh mushrooms, sliced

6.

Fish Dishes

In order for a fish to be considered kosher, it must have fins and scales. (If you have any question regarding which fish are kosher, check with your local rabbi. He can direct you to a comprehensive list of kosher varieties.) Shellfish are not kosher. A pareve food, fish may be eaten at a meal with either meat or dairy. Fish and dairy foods may be eaten together on the same plate. However, fish and meat, although permitted to be eaten at the same meal, should be served separately. It is customary to use a separate plate and eating utensils for each, although the plate and utensils need only to be washed between courses.

Fish can be a healthy part of any diet. Many fish, including tuna, salmon, and bluefish, have very high levels of valuable omega-3-fatty acids. These fatty acids have been shown to help in the reduction of blood cholesterol. They also aid in lowering blood pressure and preventing blood clot formation. The Japanese, whose diets regularly include fish, have the lowest rates of heart disease in the world.

When shopping for fish, be sure to choose the freshest available. For whole fish, choose ones with shiny skin and bright red gills that spread easily when opened. Fish fillets should have firm flesh. Fresh fish has a clean fresh scent, not a "fishy" odor. Because it is highly perishable, fish should be refrigerated and cooked the same day or shortly after it is purchased.

Cooking fish is, by definition, quick and easy. Baking and poaching are the two healthful cooking methods used in my recipes. When baking, the key is to cook the fish at a moderate temperature for a short time. The time will vary depending on the thickness of the fish. You'll know the fish is cooked when its flesh is completely opaque and it easily flakes with a fork. To prevent the fish from drying out, remove it from the heat as soon as it is cooked. Poaching is another method I use for cooking fish. Healthful and easy, poaching adds no fat and, when using a flavorful poaching liquid, imparts a wonderful flavor. (For more information, *see* Poaching Fish on page 134).

This chapter offers simple dishes such as Vegetable Baked Flounder and Cream of Mushroom Cod, as well as more elaborate creations like Seafood Lasagna and Flying Fish Pie. All are flavorful and delicious enough to satisfy your most demanding guests.

Flying Fish Pie

Yield: *8 servings*

1 1/2 pounds flounder or other thin white fish fillets, rinsed and patted dry

1 cup dry white wine

1 tablespoon Worcestershire sauce

40-ounce can yams, drained

1 large onion, thinly sliced

1 large tomato, thinly sliced

3 hard-boiled medium egg whites, thinly sliced

This tasty dish, which takes only minutes to prepare, is popular in Barbados, where flying fish is the national fish. Any thin, white fish works well in this recipe.

1. Preheat the oven to 350°F. Lightly coat a medium baking dish with olive oil cooking spray. Combine the wine and Worcestershire sauce in a small bowl and set aside.

2. Mash the yams in a large bowl, then evenly spread half on the bottom of the baking dish. Place the fish fillets on top, then add a layer of onion, tomato, and egg slices. Cover with the remaining yams and top with the wine mixture.

3. Bake uncovered for 30 minutes, or until the yams are slightly brown at the edges.

4. Spoon portions onto individual plates and enjoy piping hot.

NUTRITIONAL FACTS (PER SERVING)
Calories: 236   Fat: 0.7 g   Protein: 16.2 g   Cholesterol: 0 mg
Fiber: 5.4 g   Sodium: 171 mg   Carbohydrates: 36.1 g

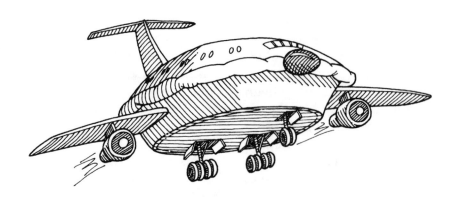

Caribbean Potted Fish

This dish, which takes less than 2 minutes to prepare and 15 minutes to cook, makes both a wonderful main dish or a tasty appetizer.

1. Preheat the oven to 350°F. Lightly coat a medium baking dish with olive oil cooking spray. Set aside.

2. Roll up each fish fillet and fasten with a toothpick.

3. Combine the flour and pepper in a small bowl. Dredge the fish rolls in the flour mixture, then arrange in the baking dish. Drizzle with olive oil.

4. Combine the vinegar and water in a small bowl and spoon over the fish. Place a bay leaf on top of each fish, and cover the dish loosely with wax paper.

5. Bake for 15 minutes, or until the fish is completely opaque and easily flakes with a fork.

6. Remove and discard the bay leaves before serving.

Yield: *8 servings*

8 fish fillets (4 ounces each) flounder, perch, and whiting are good choices

2 tablespoons whole wheat flour

1/4 teaspoon ground black pepper

1/4 cup vinegar

1/4 cup cold water

1 teaspoon olive oil

8 bay leaves

NUTRITIONAL FACTS (PER SERVING)

Calories: 90   Carbohydrates: 1.8 g   Cholesterol: 0 mg
Fat: 1.2 g   Fiber: 0.3 g   Protein: 17.2 g   Sodium: 64 mg

Seafood Lasagna

Yield: *16 servings*

16 ounces lasagna noodles

1/2 cup shredded part-skim mozzarella cheese

CHEESE FILLING

1 1/2 cups fat-free cream-style cottage cheese

8 ounces fat-free cream cheese, softened

1 large onion, finely chopped

2 tablespoons chopped fresh basil

1/8 teaspoon ground black pepper

1 medium egg white, lightly beaten

FISH FILLING

2 1/3 cups skim milk

4 garlic cloves, finely chopped

1 tablespoon whole wheat flour

1/2 cup dry white wine

8 ounces flounder or any thin white fish fillets, cubed

1 pound imitation crabmeat*

1 1/2 cups sliced mushrooms

* If imitation crabmeat is not available, increase the flounder to 1 1/2 pounds. Cut the additional pound into 2-inch pieces and coat with 1 teaspoon paprika.

This lasagna can be made in advance and simply reheated before serving. It is a good choice to serve on the Jewish holiday of Shavuous, when it is customary to eat dairy meals.

1. Preheat the oven to 350°F. Spray a 9-x-13-inch lasagna pan with olive oil cooking spray and set aside.

2. Bring a large pot of water to boil, add the lasagna noodles, and cook according to package directions.

3. While the lasagna is cooking, prepare the fillings. For the cheese mixture, combine the cottage cheese, cream cheese, onion, basil, and pepper in a medium bowl. Stir in the egg white and set aside.

4. For the fish mixture, combine the milk, garlic, and flour in a medium bowl and blend well. Stir in the wine, then add the flounder, imitation crabmeat, and mushrooms.

5. Drain the cooked lasagna noodles, rinse with cold water, and drain again.

6. Place a layer of noodles in the bottom of the baking dish. Carefully spread half the cheese mixture over the noodles, then top with another layer of noodles. Spread half the fish mixture on top. Repeat the layers, ending with a layer of noodles. Top with the mozzarella cheese.

7. Bake uncovered for 45 minutes, or until the mozzarella is melted and beginning to brown.

8. Remove the lasagna from the oven. Allow to sit 10 minutes before cutting into squares and serving.

NUTRITIONAL FACTS (PER SERVING)

Calories: 196   Carbohydrates: 25.6 g   Cholesterol: 3 mg
Fat: 0.8 g   Fiber: 1 g   Protein: 17.7 g   Sodium: 274 mg

Long Beach Cabbage Fish

In honor of my hometown.

Yield: *4 servings*

1. Preheat the oven to 350°F. Coat a medium baking dish with olive oil cooking spray and set aside.

2. Lightly coat a nonstick skillet with olive oil cooking spray and place over medium heat. Add the onion, cabbage, tomato, and 2 tablespoons of the water. Simmer 5 to 10 minutes, or until the onion is soft and begins to turn brown. Add the flour and paprika, and stir for one minute. Add the remaining water and simmer another 5 to 10 minutes, or until the cabbage is soft and tender.

3. While the cabbage mixture is simmering, brush the mayonnaise over the flounder with a pastry brush. Arrange the fillets in the baking dish and cover with the hot cabbage mixture.

4. Bake uncovered for 10 minutes, or until the fish is no longer translucent and easily flakes with a fork.

5. Transfer to a platter and serve.

1 pound flounder fillets, rinsed and patted dry

1 medium onion, coarsely chopped

1 cup chopped cabbage

1 medium tomato, diced

1/2 cup water

1 tablespoon whole wheat flour

1 1/2 tablespoons paprika

1 tablespoon fat-free mayonnaise

NUTRITIONAL FACTS (PER SERVING)

Calories: 108   Carbohydrates: 6.8 g   Cholesterol: 0 mg
Fat: 1 g   Fiber: 1.2 g   Protein: 18.1 g   Sodium: 239 mg

Vegetable Baked Flounder

Yield: *4 servings*

4 small whole flounders (8 ounces each), scaled, gutted, and heads removed

2 medium leeks

2 medium red bell peppers, seeded and coarsely chopped

1 cup sliced mushrooms

1 cup dry white wine

Although this recipe calls for flounder, feel free to use any small whole fish that are considered kosher.

1. Preheat the oven to 350°F. Lightly coat a 9-x-13-inch baking pan with olive oil cooking spray.

2. Cut the leeks in half lengthwise and rinse well. Cut away and discard the tough upper green stems. Coarsely chop the white and light green parts.

3. Place the fish in the baking dish. Cover with leeks, red peppers, and mushrooms. Top with the wine.

4. Bake uncovered for 30 minutes, or until the fish easily flakes from the bone.

5. Remove and discard the skin, carefully remove the bones, and place the fillets on a platter. Top with the vegetables and serve.

NUTRITIONAL FACTS (PER SERVING)
Calories: 139   Carbohydrates: 7.5 g   Cholesterol: 0 mg
Fat: 0.7 g   Fiber: 1.5 g   Protein: 16.1 g   Sodium: 66 mg

My Mother's Baked Codfish

A sweet and delicious fish dish with a quick cooking time.

Yield: *4 servings*

1. Preheat the oven to 350°F. Lightly coat a medium baking dish with olive oil cooking spray.

2. To make the marinade, combine the wine, water, tarragon, and bay leaf in a skillet and bring to a boil. Remove from the heat, and place in a heatproof bowl.

3. Place the fillets in the marinade and turn to coat. Refrigerate for 1 hour.

4. Remove the fillets from the marinade, pat dry, and place in the baking dish.

5. Combine the orange juice, orange rind, ginger, and white pepper in a small bowl. Spoon this mixture over the fish. Top with orange slices.

6. Bake for 20 minutes, or until the fish is completely opaque and easily flakes with a fork.

7. Place the fillets on a platter, top with orange slices, and serve.

1 pound codfish fillets, rinsed and patted dry

3/4 cup orange juice

1 tablespoon grated orange rind

1/4 teaspoon ground ginger

1/8 teaspoon ground white pepper

2 medium oranges, cut into round slices

MARINADE

1/2 cup dry white wine

1/4 cup water

1 teaspoon tarragon leaves

1 bay leaf

NUTRITIONAL FACTS (PER SERVING)
Calories: 141   Carbohydrates: 15.4 g   Cholesterol: 49 mg
Fat: 1.1 g   Fiber: 1.9 g   Protein: 21.4 g   Sodium: 63 mg

Cream of Mushroom Cod

Yield: *4 servings*

1 pound cod fillets, rinsed and
  patted dry

1 cup skim milk

1 tablespoon whole wheat flour

3/4 cup mushrooms, sliced

1 clove garlic, thinly sliced

For the sauce in this dairy dish, you can use commercial low-sodium cream of mushroom soup.

1. Preheat the oven to 350°F. Lightly coat a medium baking dish with olive oil cooking spray, and place the fish in the bottom.

2. Combine the milk and flour in a small saucepan over medium-low heat. Add the mushrooms and garlic. Stir the mixture for 3 to 5 minutes until it begins to thicken. Remove from the heat and spoon over the fish.

3. Bake uncovered for 20 to 30 minutes, or until the fish is completely opaque and easily flakes with a fork.

4. Transfer to a platter and serve.

NUTRITIONAL FACTS (PER SERVING)
Calories: 125   Carbohydrates: 5.1 g   Cholesterol: 50 mg
Fat: 1 g   Fiber: 0.4 g   Protein: 22.9 g   Sodium: 94 mg

Pasta Bean Tuna

A great one-dish meal. You can substitute the fresh tuna with 8 ounces of canned tuna in water. Omit the poaching instructions when using canned tuna.

1. Place the fish in a fish poacher or on a rack set in the bottom of a large pot. Add the wine, onion, dill weed, rosemary, parsley, and enough water to just cover the fish.

2. Cook covered over medium heat for 10 minutes, or until the fish is completely opaque and easily flakes with a fork.* Transfer the fish to a plate and refrigerate for 1 hour.

3. While the fish is chilling, bring a pot of water to a boil. Add the pasta and cook according to package directions. Drain, rinse with cold water, and drain again.

4. Combine the pasta, beans, mayonnaise, mustard, and parsley in a large bowl. Cut the chilled tuna into bite-sized pieces and add to the bowl. Mix well.

5. Serve with a fresh green salad and whole grain bread.

* Poaching time is determined by the thickness of the fish. Allow approximately 10 minutes for a 1-inch-thick piece, and 2 minutes for each additional inch.

Yield: *12 servings*

1 pound fresh tuna fillets

8 ounces ziti

8-ounce can mixed beans, rinsed and drained

1 tablespoon fat-free mayonnaise

1 teaspoon Dijon-style mustard

1 tablespoon chopped fresh parsley

POACHING LIQUID

1 cup dry white wine

1 small onion, thinly sliced

1 tablespoon chopped fresh dill weed

1 tablespoon chopped fresh rosemary

1 tablespoon chopped fresh parsley

NUTRITIONAL FACTS (PER SERVING) FOR POACHED FRESH TUNA

Calories: 189   Carbohydrates: 25.8 g   Cholesterol: 14 mg
Fat: 2.4   Fiber: 5.1 g   Protein: 15.5 g   Sodium: 35 mg

NUTRITIONAL FACTS (PER SERVING) FOR CANNED TUNA IN WATER

Calories: 179   Carbohydrates: 25.8 g   Cholesterol: 11 g
Fat: 0.9 g   Fiber: 5.1 g   Protein: 16.3 g   Sodium: 148 mg

Poaching Fish

Poaching is a healthful and easy way to cook fish. It adds no fat, and when a flavorful, seasoned liquid is used, poaching imparts a wonderful flavor to the fish.

To poach fish, you will need either a fish poacher or a rack that fits in the bottom of a large pot. A fish poacher is a specially designed elongated pot with a poaching stand inside. The stand has holes in the bottom that allow the poaching liquid to circulate. When using a rack instead of a fish poacher, choose one that fits in the pot and keeps the fish about 1 inch from the bottom. The fish should be immersed in the poaching liquid.

After the fish is placed in the poacher or on a rack and set in the bottom of the pot, the poaching liquid is added along with enough water to just cover the fish. The pot is then covered and placed over medium heat. The thickness of the fish will determine its cooking time. Allow approximately 10 minutes for a 1-inch-thick piece; for each additional inch, add 2 minutes cooking time. The fish is done when it is completely opaque and easily flakes with a fork.

The following poaching liquid is good for most fish varieties. The only ingredient I tend to alter is the wine. I use a red wine for less-flavorful fish like carp and whitefish, and a white wine for more flavorful varieties, such as red snapper and flounder.

1 cup dry white or red wine
1 small onion, thinly sliced
1 tablespoon chopped fresh dill weed
1 tablespoon chopped fresh rosemary
1 tablespoon chopped fresh parsley

Top Left and Center Right:
Tropical Chicken Salad (page 119)
Top Right: Flying Fish Pie (page 126)
Left: No-Cook Cold Melon Soup (page 65)

Top Right: Baked Butternut Squash (page 155)
Center: Chicken with Potatoes Lyonnaise (page 104)
Bottom: Baked Portabella Mushrooms (page 176)

Red Snapper with Yogurt-Dill Sauce

The dill sauce for this fish is considered dairy. Dried herbs can be easily substituted for the fresh.

1. Place the fish in a fish poacher or on a rack set in the bottom of a large pot. Add the wine, onion, dill weed, rosemary, parsley, and enough water to just cover the fish.

2. Place the pot over medium heat and cook covered for 10 minutes, or until the fish is completely opaque and easily flakes with a fork.* Transfer the fish to a plate and refrigerate for 1 hour.

3. To prepare the sauce, combine the ingredients in a small bowl and mix well. Cover and refrigerate.

4. Top the chilled red snappers with dill sauce or serve it on the side.

* Poaching time is determined by the thickness of the fish. Allow approximately 10 minutes for a 1-inch-thick piece, and 2 minutes for each additional inch.

NUTRITIONAL FACTS (PER SERVING)

Calories: 77   Carbohydrates: 4.9 g   Cholesterol: 17 mg
Fat: 0.7 g   Fiber: 0 g   Protein: 12.1 g   Sodium: 72 mg

VARIATION

- To enjoy this dish as a fish salad, remove the cooked fish from the bones and mix it with the yogurt-dill sauce. Serve on a bed of lettuce.

Yield: *4 servings*

2 whole red snappers (1 pound each), scaled and gutted

POACHING LIQUID

1 cup dry white wine

1 small onion, thinly sliced

1 tablespoon chopped fresh dill weed

1 tablespoon chopped fresh rosemary

1 tablespoon chopped fresh parsley

YOGURT-DILL SAUCE

1 cup plain nonfat yogurt

1 tablespoon chopped fresh dill weed

1 teaspoon finely chopped onion

1 teaspoon chopped fresh parsley

Cold Poached Salmon with Sweet Dill Sauce

Yield: *4 servings*

1 pound salmon fillets

POACHING LIQUID

1 cup dry white wine

1 small onion, thinly sliced

1 tablespoon chopped fresh
   dill weed

1 tablespoon chopped fresh
   rosemary leaves

1 tablespoon chopped fresh
   parsley

SWEET DILL SAUCE

1 cup plain nonfat yogurt

2 tablespoons chopped fresh
   dill weed

2 tablespoons fat-free Thousand
   Island salad dressing

Although salmon is considered a "fatty" fish, its saturated fat content is only 0.7 grams per serving. Salmon also contains a large amount of beneficial omega-3 fatty acids.

1. Place the fish in a fish poacher or on a rack set in the bottom of a large pot.

2. Place the pot over medium heat and cook covered for 10 minutes, or until the fish is completely opaque and easily flakes with a fork.* Transfer the fish to a plate and refrigerate for 1 hour.

3. To prepare the sauce, combine the ingredients in a small bowl and mix well. Cover and refrigerate.

4. Top the chilled salmon with dill sauce or serve it on the side.

* Poaching time is determined by the thickness of the fish. Allow approximately 10 minutes for a 1-inch-thick piece, and 2 minutes for each additional inch.

NUTRITIONAL FACTS (PER SERVING)
Calories: 175   Carbohydrates: 6.7 g   Cholesterol: 60 mg
Fat: 4.1 g   Fiber: 0 g   Protein: 26.2 g   Sodium: 194 mg

7.
Turkey Dishes

Skinless, white meat turkey is a great choice for healthy low-fat meals. Much lower in fat than beef and other meats, turkey is even leaner than chicken. Like all meats and poultry, kosher turkeys are soaked and salted according to the laws of *kashrus.*

Skinless, boneless turkey roasts, turkey London broils, turkey breast cutlets, and ground turkey are called for in the following recipes. Be sure to trim any visible fat from the roasts and cutlets. When using ground turkey, be sure it is made from skinless white meat only. Turkey is a wonderful substitute for beef and veal in most dishes; it has a lower fat content, contains fewer calories, and requires a shorter cooking time. Unfortunately, lean turkey also has a reputation for being dry and somewhat bland. When properly combined with the right blend of sauces, spices, and other flavorful ingredients, and coupled with proper cooking methods, simple turkey can be transformed into a moist, tender, and delicious food.

I find that covering a turkey roast with bread that has been soaked in flavorful soup or juice before placing it in the oven, helps keep the meat moist and tender. Keeping the oven temperature at a moderate 350°F is another important factor in preventing the turkey from drying out. If you have the time, cook turkey at an even lower 250°F to 300°F for a longer period of time. This will result in turkey that is even moister and more tender.

For the ground meat dishes in this chapter, I use only ground white meat turkey, but feel free to replace this with ground chicken, veal, or any combination thereof. Although not as low in fat as ground turkey, ground white meat chicken and veal are other good choices. Combining ground turkey with other ground meats adds flavor to the mixture while keeping the fat content relatively low. Looking for a vegetarian version? Use TVP (texturized vegetable protein) or vegetable protein crumbles—healthy, fat-free substitutes for ground meat. A pareve food, these ground meat alternatives can be combined with a variety of dairy ingredients, including fat-free or low-fat cheeses. Green Giant makes a kosher vegetable protein product that is readily available in many supermarkets.

You may be surprised to discover just how moist and delectable the following turkey dishes are. You will be proud to serve them.

Apricot Turkey Roast

Yield: *8 servings*

2-pound skinless, boneless white meat turkey roast

3 tablespoons unsweetened apricot preserves

1 cup reconstituted dried onion soup mix

6 slices day-old challah or white bread

Follow the simple steps below for a turkey roast that is amazingly moist and tender.

1. Preheat the oven to 350°F. Lightly coat a medium baking dish with olive oil cooking spray.

2. Place the turkey in the baking dish and cover it with the apricot preserves.

3. Soak each slice of bread with onion soup. Completely cover the turkey with the bread.

4. Bake for 1 hour, or until the juices from the turkey run clear. The center of the roast should be slightly pink.

5. Mash the bread and serve it with slices of the roasted turkey.

NUTRITIONAL FACTS (PER SERVING)
Calories: 168   Carbohydrates: 15.1 g   Cholesterol: 49 mg
Fat: 2.2 g   Fiber: 0.7g   Protein: 21 g   Sodium: 286 mg

VARIATIONS

- Try substituting a veal roast for the turkey. Cooking time is about the same.

- Use cubed veal stew meat instead of turkey. Cooking time is only 30 minutes.

NUTRITIONAL FACTS (PER SERVING) WITH VEAL
Calories: 199   Carbohydrates: 15.1 g   Cholesterol: 96 mg
Fat: 3.8 g   Fiber: 0.7 g   Protein: 25.1 g   Sodium: 330 mg

Tomato-Rice Turkey

The turkey stays moist and tender as it cooks beneath the tomato-rice sauce.

1. Bring 1¼ cups of water to boil in a small saucepan. Stir in the rice, reduce the heat to low, and cover. Cook for 35 minutes, or until the rice is tender and easily fluffs with a fork.

2. Preheat the oven to 350°F. Coat a 9-x-13-inch baking dish with olive oil cooking spray and set aside.

3. Lightly coat a nonstick skillet with cooking spray. Add the tomatoes, onion, water, and cooked rice, and bring to a boil. Stir in the basil and black pepper. Remove from the heat.

4. Cut the turkey into 1-inch pieces and place in the baking dish. Sprinkle with paprika. Spoon the tomato-rice mixture over the turkey.

5. Bake for 30 minutes, stirring occasionally until the turkey pieces are completely opaque.

6. Spoon into a large bowl and serve hot.

Yield: *8 servings*

2 pounds turkey breast cutlets

½ cup brown rice

28-ounce can no-sodium crushed tomatoes

1 medium onion, coarsely chopped

¼ cups water

1 tablespoon chopped fresh basil

⅛ teaspoon ground black pepper

1 teaspoon paprika

NUTRITIONAL FACTS (PER SERVING)

Calories: 162   Carbohydrates: 14.6 g   Cholesterol: 48 mg
Fat: 1.9 g   Fiber: 2.3 g   Protein: 21.1 g   Sodium: 134 mg

VARIATION

- To reduce the cooking time, use instant rice instead of the longer-cooking variety.

My Mother's Microwave Turkey Roast

Yield: *8 servings*

2-pound skinless, boneless white meat turkey roast

1 cup Homemade Cranberry Sauce (page 167), or 8-ounce can commercial variety

1 tablespoon dry onion soup mix

This simple meal takes less than 30 minutes to prepare from start to finish.

1. Place the turkey in a microwave-safe baking dish.

2. Combine the cranberry sauce and onion soup mix in a small bowl. Spoon over the turkey to completely cover.

3. If your microwave has a temperature probe, insert it horizontally into the thickest part of the roast. Set the temperature to 140°F at power level 8 (80 percent of full power). Cook for 20 minutes, or until the temperature of the turkey reaches 140°F. If you are not using a temperature probe, cook the turkey until its juices run clear.

4. Cut the turkey into slices and serve over brown rice or pasta.

NUTRITIONAL FACTS (PER SERVING)

Calories: 141   Carbohydrates: 12 g   Cholesterol: 48 mg
Fat: 1.4 g   Fiber: 0.5 g   Protein: 19.3 g   Sodium: 225 mg

The Secret for Moist, Tender Turkey

Lean turkey, although very low in fat, also has the reputation for being somewhat dry. Proper cooking is the secret for moist, tender roasted turkey every time. Before placing the roast in the oven, cover it with flavorful soup- or juice-soaked bread. And keep the oven temperature at a moderate 350°F. If you have the time, cook the turkey at an even lower 250°F or 300°F for a longer period of time.

Orange-Strawberry Turkey Roast

This roast is covered in orange juice-soaked bread as it cooks. It is one of my favorites.

1. Preheat the oven to 350°F. Lightly coat a 9-x-13-inch baking dish with olive oil cooking spray.

2. Place the turkey in the baking dish. Sprinkle with mint, thyme, and sage, then cover with strawberry preserves. Spoon ½ cup of the orange juice over the roast.

3. Pour 1½ cups of the orange juice into a bowl. Soak each slice of bread with the juice. Completely cover the turkey with the bread.

4. Bake uncovered for 1 hour, then spoon the remaining orange juice over the bread. Continue to cook another 15 to 30 minutes, or until the juices from the turkey run clear. The center of the roast should be slightly pink.

5. Remove the bread and place it in a bowl. Mash it and serve along with slices of the roasted turkey.

Yield: *8 servings*

2-pound skinless, boneless white meat turkey roast

2 tablespoons chopped fresh mint leaves

2 tablespoons chopped fresh thyme

2 tablespoons fresh whole sage

¼ cup unsweetened strawberry preserves

3 cups orange juice

6 slices day-old challah or white bread

NUTRITIONAL FACTS (PER SERVING)
Calories: 201   Carbohydrates: 26.6 g   Cholesterol: 49 mg
Fat: 2.3 g   Fiber: 1 g   Protein: 21.5 g   Sodium: 158 mg

The Bad News About Brisket

A slow-cooked beef brisket is traditionally served on the Sabbath and many holidays. Beef, however, contains large amounts of saturated fat, making it a poor nutritional choice. Typically, beef brisket contains almost 400 calories and over 30 grams of fat per serving.

Although other lean beef cuts may be lower in fat than brisket, their fat content is still fairly high. If, however, you would like to make an occasional potted beef dish, be sure to use the leanest possible cuts of kosher-certified beef such as silver tip roast or London broil. Better yet, instead of beef, try a veal or white meat turkey roast. Nutritional analysis for all of these options are provided below.

Aunt Helen's Potted Beef Roast

Yield: *8 servings*

2 medium carrot, peeled and cut into 2-inch slices

1 large onion, thinly sliced

3 tablespoons water

2-pound silver tip roast or London broil, trimmed of any visible fat

1 1/2 tablespoons dry onion soup mix

1 teaspoon paprika

1/2 teaspoon ground black pepper

1/2 cup dry red wine

3 tablespoons low-sodium ketchup

1. Coat a medium skillet with olive oil cooking spray. Add the carrots, onions, and 1 tablespoon of water. Cook over medium heat for 5 minutes, stirring frequently. Add the meat to the skillet, brown 5 minutes on each side.

2. Transfer skillet ingredients to a 6-quart Dutch oven that is coated with olive oil cooking spray. Sprinkle the soup mix, paprika, and black pepper over the meat. Top with wine, ketchup, and remaining water.

3. Cover and cook over low heat for 1 hour. Remove the meat, cut into thin slices, and return to the pot. Cover and cook another 30 minutes.

4. Arrange the meat slices on a platter. Surround with carrots and onions.

NUTRITIONAL FACTS (PER SERVING)
FOR SILVER TIP BEEF ROAST

Calories: 292   Carbohydrates: 6 g   Cholesterol: 102 mg
Fat: 10 g   Fiber: 1.3 g   Protein: 40.1 g   Sodium: 376 mg

NUTRITIONAL FACTS (PER SERVING) FOR VEAL ROAST

Calories: 161   Carbohydrates: 6 g   Cholesterol: 95 mg
Fat: 3.1 g   Fiber: 1.3 g   Protein: 23.8 g   Sodium: 420 mg

NUTRITIONAL FACTS (PER SERVING)
FOR WHITE MEAT TURKEY ROAST

Calories: 130   Carbohydrates: 6 g   Cholesterol: 48 mg
Fat: 1.6 g   Fiber: 1.3 g   Protein: 19.8 g   Sodium: 376 mg

Baked Turkey with Strawberry Sauce

If fresh strawberries are not in season, you can use 1 cup frozen thawed strawberries with equally good results.

Yield: *8 servings*

1. Preheat the oven to 350°F. Lightly coat a 9-x-13-inch baking dish with olive-oil cooking spray.

2. Spread the brown rice evenly over the bottom of the baking dish. Lay the turkey pieces on top and sprinkle with cinnamon and rosemary. Place in the oven.

3. Place the strawberries, sugar, and lemon juice in a food processor or blender. Purée until smooth and set aside.

4. After the turkey has been cooking for 20 minutes, cover it with the strawberry sauce. Continue to bake another 10 minutes, or until the turkey is no longer pink.

5. Transfer to a platter and serve.

1 cup cooked brown rice

2 pounds turkey breast cutlets, cut into bite-sized pieces

2 tablespoons ground cinnamon

1 tablespoon rosemary

STRAWBERRY SAUCE

1 pint fresh strawberries, hulled and cut in half

¹/₄ cup sugar

1 tablespoon lemon juice

NUTRITIONAL FACTS (PER SERVING)

Calories: 161   Carbohydrates: 16.2 g   Cholesterol: 48 mg
Fat: 1.7 g   Fiber: 1.7 g   Protein: 19.9 g   Sodium: 52 mg

Long Beach Stuffed Peppers

Yield: *8 servings*

1 cup brown rice

8 large red, green, and/or yellow bell peppers

1½ pounds ground white meat turkey

½ teaspoon ground black pepper

16-ounce can no-sodium tomato sauce

16-ounce can no-sodium tomato soup

2 cups water

1 teaspoon granulated brown sugar

Use red, green, and yellow bell peppers for a colorful presentation.

1. Bring 2½ cups of water to boil in a small saucepan. Stir in the rice, reduce the heat to low, and cover. Cook for 30 minutes, or until the rice is tender and easily fluffs with a fork.

2. While the rice cooks, wash the peppers and place in a microwave-safe baking dish. Cover with wax paper and microwave for 1½ minutes on High. When the peppers are cool enough to handle, cut away the stems and remove the seeds.

3. Combine the rice, turkey, black pepper, and half the tomato sauce in a bowl. Mix well and spoon into the peppers.

4. Bring the tomato soup, water, and the remaining tomato sauce to a boil in a large pot. Reduce the heat to low and carefully add the stuffed peppers. Cover and simmer for 1 hour, or until the turkey is no longer pink. When the peppers are just about cooked, sprinkle them with brown sugar.

5. Before serving, spoon some of the sauce over each pepper.

NUTRITIONAL FACTS (PER PEPPER)
Calories: 201   Carbohydrates: 28 g   Cholesterol: 36 mg
Fat: 1.7 g   Fiber: 1.1 g   Protein: 18.4 g   Sodium: 61 mg

VARIATIONS

• To reduce the cooking time, use instant rice instead of the longer-cooking variety.

• For a vegetarian version, use 12 ounces vegetable protein crumbles instead of ground turkey. Simmer for 40 minutes, or until the crumbles are soft.

NUTRITIONAL FACTS (PER PEPPER)
WITH VEGETABLE PROTEIN CRUMBLES
Calories: 196   Carbohydrates: 33.7 g   Cholesterol: 0 mg
Fat: 0.8 g   Fiber: 5.2 g   Protein: 14.2 g   Sodium: 212 mg

Fiesta Bake

A dish your whole family will love.

1. Preheat the oven to 350°F. Lightly coat a 9-x-13-inch baking dish with olive oil cooking spray and set aside.

2. Combine the turkey, tomato sauce, and salsa in a bowl. Add the onion and corn kernels, and mix well. Spoon this mixture into the baking dish, spreading it evenly.

3. Bake for 40 minutes, or until the turkey is no longer pink.

4. Spoon into bowls and top with lettuce, tomato, and nondairy soy cheese, if using.

Yield: 8 servings

1 1/2 pounds ground white meat turkey

8-ounce can no-sodium tomato sauce

1/2 cup Fresh Homemade Salsa (page 34), or low-sodium commercial variety)

1 medium onion, finely chopped

1 cup corn kernels

4 cups shredded lettuce

1 large tomato, coarsely chopped

Nondairy soy cheese (optional)

NUTRITIONAL FACTS (PER SERVING)
Calories: 113   Carbohydrates: 8.3 g   Cholesterol: 36 mg
Fat: 1.9 g Fiber: 1.5 g   Protein: 16 g   Sodium: 128 mg

VARIATION

• For a vegetarian filling, use 12 ounces vegetable protein crumbles instead of ground turkey. Bake for 30 minutes, or until the crumbles are soft. Vegetable protein crumbles are pareve, and may be topped with shredded nonfat cheese.

NUTRITIONAL FACTS (PER SERVING)
WITH VEGETABLE PROTEIN CRUMBLES
Calories: 91   Carbohydrates: 14 g   Cholesterol: 0 mg
Fat: 0.1 g   Fiber: 4.8 g   Protein: 11.1 g   Sodium: 266 mg

Turkish Meat Pie

Yield: *8 servings*

3 sheets of matzoh

1½ pounds ground white meat turkey

1 cup sweet red wine

3 medium egg whites

2 tablespoons ground cinnamon

¼ teaspoon ground black pepper

Passover is the celebration of the freedom of the Children of Israel from slavery. During this holiday, only unleavened bread—matzoh—may be eaten. There are many traditional recipes found in Jewish communities around the world that utilize matzohs in interesting ways. This pie is a variation of an unusual sweet meat dish of Sephardic origin.

1. Preheat the oven to 350°F. Coat the bottom and sides of a 9-x-13-inch baking dish with olive oil cooking spray.

2. Place 1½ sheets of the matzoh in a large shallow dish. Pour just enough boiling water over the matzohs to make them soft and pliable, but not so soft that they fall apart.

3. Pat the matzohs with paper towels to remove any excess water, then use them to line the bottom and sides of the baking dish.

4. Combine the turkey, wine, egg whites, cinnamon, and black pepper in a bowl. Spoon this mixture in an even layer on top of the matzoh.

5. Soften the remaining matzohs and use them to cover the turkey mixture.

6. Bake for 1 hour, or until the matzoh is lightly brown.

7. Allow to sit 5 minutes before cutting into squares and serving.

NUTRITIONAL FACTS (PER SERVING)

Calories: 168   Carbohydrates: 14 g   Cholesterol: 36 mg
Fat: 1.2 g   Fiber: 1.3 g   Protein: 16.8 g   Sodium: 62 mg

VARIATION

- For a vegetarian version, use 12 ounces vegetable protein crumbles instead of ground turkey. Bake for 40 minutes, or until the crumbles are soft.

NUTRITIONAL FACTS (PER SERVING)
WITH VEGETABLE PROTEIN CRUMBLES

Calories: 164   Carbohydrates: 19.7 g   Cholesterol: 0 mg
Fat: 0.2 g   Fiber: 5.3 g   Protein: 12.5 g   Sodium: 213 mg

Turkey Bean Bake

Serve this dish over mashed potatoes for a real homestyle meal.

Yield: *8 servings*

1. Preheat the oven to 350°F. Lightly coat a medium baking dish with olive oil cooking spray. Place the turkey in the baking dish.

2. Combine the remaining ingredients in a bowl and spoon over the turkey.

3. Bake for 1 to 1½ hours (40 to 50 minutes for London broil), or until the turkey juices run clear.

4. Slice the roast and serve with the beans and sauce.

2-pound skinless, boneless white meat turkey roast, or turkey London broil

2 cups cooked red kidney beans

12-ounce can no-sodium whole tomatoes

8-ounce can no-sodium tomato sauce

1 tablespoon chopped fresh parsley

NUTRITIONAL FACTS (PER SERVING)

Calories: 166   Carbohydrates: 13.5 g   Cholesterol: 48 mg
Fat: 1.6 g   Fiber: 4.1 g   Protein: 23.8 g   Sodium: 64 mg

Turkey Tofu Tumble

Yield: *8 servings*

1 pound ground white meat
  turkey

8 ounces firm tofu

16-ounce can no-sodium tomato
  sauce

1 cup sliced mushrooms

1 medium red bell pepper,
  seeded and coarsely
  chopped

1 medium green bell pepper,
  seeded and coarsely
  chopped

1 tablespoon chopped fresh
  basil

1 teaspoon chopped fresh
  rosemary

1/8 teaspoon oregano

Tofu has a wonderful ability to absorb the flavors of its surrounding ingredients. It adds both texture and moistness to this dish.

1. Preheat the oven to 350°F. Spray a medium baking dish with olive oil cooking spray.

2. Pat the tofu dry with paper towels, then crumble it into a bowl. Add the turkey and mix with the tofu.

3. In another bowl, combine all of the remaining ingredients, then add to the turkey-tofu mixture. Mix gently, then place in the baking dish. Pat into an even layer.

4. Bake for 40 minutes or until the turkey is no longer pink.

5. Cut into squares and serve with warm, crusty Italian bread.

NUTRITIONAL FACTS (PER SERVING)
Calories: 90   Carbohydrates: 5.2 g   Cholesterol: 24 mg
Fat: 2.1 g   Fiber: 0.9 g   Protein: 13.1 g   Sodium: 37 mg

Jamaican Jerk Turkey

Usually used to flavor chicken, Jamaican jerk sauce really livens up this grilled turkey dish.

Yield: *8 servings*

1. Place the turkey in a baking dish or bowl and set aside.

2. Add the onion, garlic, jalapeño pepper, and thyme to a food processor or blender. Process for 5 seconds, or until very smooth. Transfer mixture to a bowl along with the remaining ingredients. Mix well and pour over the turkey. Marinate for 1 hour in the refrigerator.

3. Place the marinated turkey on a charcoal or gas grill over medium heat (about 6 to 8 inches above the heat source). Cover and grill for 10 minutes, then turn over and cook an additional 10 minutes, or until the turkey is no longer pink inside.

4. Thinly slice the turkey, and serve.

2-pound turkey London broil

1 medium onion, cut into chunks

2 garlic cloves

1 medium jalapeño pepper, seeded

1 tablespoon chopped fresh thyme

2 tablespoons lime juice

2 tablespoons rum

2 tablespoons granulated brown sugar

1 tablespoon low-sodium soy sauce

1 tablespoon ground allspice

NUTRITIONAL FACTS (PER SERVING)
Calories: 122   Carbohydrates: 5.2 g   Cholesterol: 48 mg
Fat: 1.4 g   Fiber: 0.7 g   Protein: 19.5 g   Sodium: 187 mg

8.

Vegetarian Side Dishes

Fresh vegetables, grains, and legumes play an increasingly important role in today's healthy eating, elevating what was once the simple side dish to new heights. No longer just a boring canned or frozen vegetable that is upstaged by the main course, the side dish has taken on a significant supporting role—a tasty yet nutritional enhancement to a complete meal.

Vegetables, which are a vital part of a healthy diet, play a starring role in most of my side dishes. I use lots of green leafy vegetables as well as yellow and orange varieties, which are high in vitamins and carotenoids. Carotenoids are a class of compounds related to vitamin A. The best known is beta-carotene. Carotenoids may be responsible for aiding in cancer prevention by neutralizing free radicals. My side dishes also include cruciferous vegetables, such as broccoli, cauliflower, and Brussels sprouts, which are believed to have cancer-preventive properties.

According to Jewish law, all natural products, such as fruits, vegetables, and grains, are considered kosher. However, natural

foods that have been processed must be checked for kosher certification. All fresh vegetables and fruits must be carefully inspected for insects and washed well prior to cooking or eating.

COOKING VEGETABLES

Never has cooking with vegetables been easier. Readily available fresh produce can be found in great abundance and in wide varieties on most supermarket shelves. In addition, bags of precut items such as broccoli florets and baby carrots help cut back on a recipe's preparation time. Even salads come precut and packaged.

In addition to being nutritionally sound, all of the dishes presented in this chapter have another thing in common—ease of preparation. They can be put together quickly and don't require much fuss, leaving you free to do other things as the dish cooks.

Most of the recipes in this chapter call for fresh vegetables, but you can substitute frozen or canned varieties if you choose.

When buying canned or frozen vegetables, be sure to the check labels for kosher certification and choose only low-sodium brands.

Steaming Methods

Steaming vegetables is a superior method to boiling, which cooks away valuable vitamins and minerals. Steaming preserves the vitamin content and the vibrant color of most vegetables. You can steam vegetables on the stovetop or in the microwave.

A special plastic steamer for microwaves is a convenient item. It is a plastic bowl with small holes that fits into a larger bowl with a cover. When the water in the bottom of the larger bowl begins to boil, the steam circulates through the holes and cooks the vegetables.

Bamboo steamer baskets and adjustable metal steamer inserts are used to cook vegetables on the stovetop. These steamers, which hold the vegetables, are placed in large pots with an inch or so of boiling water. The pot is covered and the vegetables are steamed until tender.

Steaming Vegetables in the Microwave

While a steamer is a convenient utensil to use for cooking vegetables in the microwave, it isn't necessary. If you don't have a steamer, simply place the fresh vegetables in a microwave-safe bowl. Add a tablespoon of water, cover with wax paper, and microwave until the vegetables are tender. Nothing could be easier. When steaming frozen vegetables, use the same method, only without the added water.

When microwaving vegetables in their entirety, such as potatoes and squash, poke a number of holes in the skin with a fork or knife. This will prevent the whole vegetable from exploding due to internal steam buildup. It also allows the heat to circulate evenly.

About Sautéing

Many dishes such as stews and casseroles require precooked vegetables. Sautéing, one popular method for precooking, requires oil as well as time. Generally, I have found sautéing to be an unnecessary step. Why add fat and calories when you don't have to? In stews and baked dishes, vegetables become tender without the need for precooking. And for those dishes in which cooked vegetables are a must, I simply steam them in the microwave. Cooking vegetables in the microwave is also quicker and easier than cooking them on the stovetop, which requires constant attention to prevent burning. And as an added bonus, cleanup is a snap. It's much easier to clean a bowl that has held vegetables and water, than it is to clean an oily skillet.

If you want the taste of vegetables that have been sautéed in oil, simply spray the bowl, with an olive oil cooking spray before adding the vegetables. A light coating of cooking spray adds an insignificant amount of fat and almost no calories. For those who do not have a microwave and must precook vegetables on the stovetop, simply substitute the oil with cooking spray and use a nonstick skillet.

From vegetable casseroles and pasta salads to the traditional tsimmes and kugel dishes, this chapter is bursting with great accompaniments for your entrées. All are delicious, healthful, and easy to prepare.

Oven-Fried Dirty Potatoes

Much of a potato's vitamin content lies just under the skin, which is a good reason for not peeling it. The "dirty" in this recipe title refers to the fact that the potatoes are cooked with their skins on.

1. Preheat the oven to 425°F. Scrub the potatoes well, cut into 1/4-inch slices, and pat dry with paper towels.

2. Place the potato slices in a plastic resealable bag. Add the olive oil, paprika, garlic powder, parsley, and black pepper. Seal the bag and shake to coat the potatoes evenly.

3. Arrange the potatoes on an ungreased baking sheet and bake for 20 minutes, turning the slices once as they bake.

4. Serve hot.

Yield: *10 servings*

6 large potatoes, unpeeled

1 teaspoon olive oil

1/2 teaspoon paprika

1/2 teaspoon garlic powder

1 teaspoon chopped fresh parsley

1/8 teaspoon ground black pepper

NUTRITIONAL FACTS (PER SERVING)
Calories: 45   Carbohydrates: 9.3 g   Cholesterol: 0 mg
Fat: 0.5 g   Fiber: 0.8 g   Protein: 1.1 g   Sodium: 4 mg

Sweet Acorn Squash

Yield: *4 servings*

1 large acorn squash

1 tablespoon honey

1 teaspoon ground cinnamon

$1/8$ teaspoon ground nutmeg

Using a knife or fork, be sure to poke holes in the skin of a whole squash before cooking it in the microwave. This will prevent the squash from exploding and allow it to cook evenly.

1. Preheat the oven to 350°F. After poking holes in the squash, place it in a shallow baking dish that has been lightly coated with olive oil cooking spray

2. Bake uncovered for 1 hour. Remove the squash from the oven, carefully slice in half, and discard the seeds. Spoon honey over the halves and sprinkle with cinnamon and nutmeg.

3. Put the squash halves back together and return to the oven for 10 minutes, or until the squash is tender.

4. Allow the squash to cool 10 minutes. Using a spoon, scoop the squash from its shell and place in a serving bowl. Enjoy hot.

NUTRITIONAL FACTS (PER SERVING)

Calories: 51   Carbohydrates: 13.4 g   Cholesterol: 0 mg
Fat: 0.1 g   Fiber: 0.3 g   Protein: 0.7 g   Sodium: 3 mg

VARIATION

- To cook this dish in the microwave, place the squash in a microwave-safe bowl. Cover with wax paper and cook for 6 minutes on High. After cutting, seeding, and adding the honey, cinnamon, and nutmeg, put the halves back together and cook another 2 minutes.

Baked Butternut Squash

A very simple and very delicious side dish.

Yield: *6 servings*

1. Preheat the oven to 350°F. Coat a medium baking dish with olive oil cooking spray.

2. Layer the squash slices in the baking dish. Spoon the honey over the squash and sprinkle with cinnamon.

3. Bake uncovered for 1 hour, or until the squash is tender.

4. Transfer to a serving platter and enjoy hot.

1 large butternut squash, seeded and cut into 1-inch round slices

1 tablespoon honey

$\frac{1}{2}$ teaspoon ground cinnamon

NUTRITIONAL FACTS (PER SERVING)

Calories: 54   Carbohydrates: 14.2 g   Cholesterol: 0 mg
Fat: 0.1 g   Fiber: 0.1 g   Protein: 1 g   Sodium: 4 mg

VARIATION

• To cook this dish in the microwave, place the prepared squash in a microwave-safe bowl. Cook for 7 minutes on High, or until the squash is tender.

Spiced Acorn Squash

Yield: *10 servings*

4 medium acorn squash

1 tablespoon granulated brown sugar

1 teaspoon ground cinnamon

3/4 teaspoon ground ginger

1/4 teaspoon ground mace

1 tablespoon apple cider vinegar

If you find it hard to cut the uncooked squash in half, you may have to soften it a little first. After poking holes in the squash with a knife or fork, cook it in the microwave for 3 minutes on High. This should soften the squash enough to make cutting easy.

1. Preheat the oven to 350°F. Lightly coat a 9-x-13-inch baking dish with olive oil cooking spray.

2. Cut each squash in half, remove and discard the seeds, then place the halves in the baking dish.

3. Combine the brown sugar, cinnamon, ginger, and mace in a small bowl. Sprinkle over the squash, then spoon the apple cider vinegar on top.

4. Bake covered for 1½ hours, or until the squash is tender.

5. Allow the squash to cool 10 minutes. Using a spoon, scoop the squash from its shell and place in a serving bowl. Enjoy hot.

NUTRITIONAL FACTS (PER SERVING)
Calories: 57   Carbohydrates: 14.9 g   Cholesterol: 0 mg
Fat: 0.2 g   Fiber: 0.2 g   Protein: 1.1 g   Sodium: 4 mg

VARIATION

- To cook this dish in the microwave, place 4 squash halves at a time in a microwave-safe bowl. After topping with the brown sugar mixture and vinegar, cover with wax paper and microwave for 8 to 10 minutes on High.

Sweetly Spiced Spaghetti Squash

Uncooked spaghetti squash, like acorn squash, may be hard to cut in half. To soften the squash, poke holes in it with a knife or fork, then cook it in the microwave for 3 minutes on High.

Yield: *6 servings*

1 large spaghetti squash

1 tablespoon granulated brown sugar

1 teaspoon ground cinnamon

$1/8$ teaspoon ground nutmeg

6 allspice berries

4 cloves

1. Preheat the oven to 350°F. Coat a 9-x-13-inch baking dish with olive oil cooking spray.

2. Cut the squash in half, remove and discard the seeds, then place in the baking dish.

3. Combine the brown sugar, cinnamon, nutmeg, allspice, and cloves in a small bowl. Divide mixture evenly over the squash halves.

4. Bake covered for 1 hour, or until the squash is tender.

5. Discard the allspice berries and cloves, arrange the squash halves on a platter, and serve.

NUTRITIONAL FACTS (PER SERVING)
Calories: 11   Carbohydrates: 2.6 g   Cholesterol: 0 mg
Fat: 0.1 g   Fiber: 0.2 g   Protein: 0.1 g   Sodium: 3 mg

VARIATION

- To cook this dish in the microwave, place the squash halves in a microwave-safe bowl. After topping with the brown sugar mixture, cover with wax paper and microwave for 8 minutes on High.

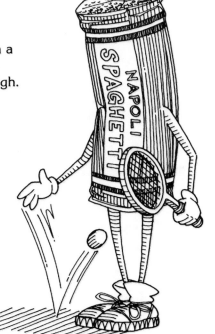

Cynthia's Broccoli Kugel

Yield: 10 servings

12 ounces "no-yolk" egg noodles

2¼ cups chopped fresh broccoli*

3 medium egg whites

1 cup skim milk

3 tablespoons unsweetened applesauce

1 medium onion, coarsely chopped

2 tablespoons dried onion soup mix

* Can use 10-ounce package frozen broccoli. Microwave for 4 minutes on High to cook, then drain.

This recipe, which is made with milk, can be served with dairy or pareve foods. To enjoy this dish with meat, use ½ cup light nondairy creamer mixed with ½ cup water instead of milk.

1. Preheat the oven to 350°F. Coat a 9-x-13-inch baking dish with olive oil cooking spray and set aside.

2. Bring 6 cups of water to boil in a large saucepan. Add the noodles, and cook according to package directions.

3. While the noodles are cooking, place the broccoli in a microwave-safe bowl, cover with wax paper, and microwave for 7 minutes on High, or until the broccoli is just tender.

4. Combine the egg whites, milk, applesauce, onion, and soup mix in a large bowl. Stir in the broccoli and cooked noodles. Spoon the mixture into the baking dish.

5. Bake for 1 hour, or until the top is lightly browned.

6. Cut into squares and serve hot or cold.

NUTRITIONAL FACTS (PER SERVING)
Calories: 163   Carbohydrates: 29.7 g   Cholesterol: 1 mg
Fat: 0.6 g   Fiber: 3.2 g   Protein: 8.7 g   Sodium: 375 mg

Potato Kugel

A traditional Sabbath dish, potato kugel is typically made with chicken fat. You will be pleasantly surprised by this fat-free version.

1. Preheat the oven to 350°F. Coat a shallow 9-x-13-inch baking dish with olive oil cooking spray and set aside.

2. Place the potatoes and onions in a food processor or blender and finely chop. Transfer to a large bowl and add the remaining ingredients. Mix well and spoon into the baking dish.

3. Bake uncovered for 40 minutes, or until the top is brown.

4. Allow to sit 5 minutes before cutting into squares and serving.

Yield: *10 servings*

6 medium baking potatoes, peeled and cut into large chunks

2 onions, cut into large chunks

3 tablespoons unsweetened applesauce

4 medium egg whites

1/2 cup whole wheat flour

1 1/2 teaspoons baking powder

1/4 teaspoon ground black pepper

NUTRITIONAL FACTS (PER SERVING)

Calories: 75 Carbohydrates: 15.5 g Cholesterol: 0 mg
Fat: 0.2 g Fiber: 2 g Protein: 3.5 g Sodium: 190 mg

VARIATION

• For an interesting flavor, add a 10-ounce package of frozen cauliflower that has been thawed and drained to the potato mixture.

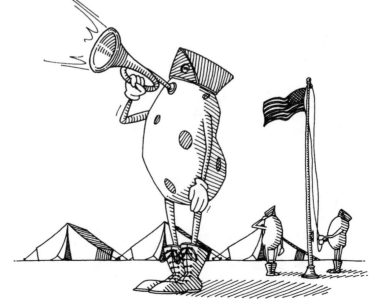

Jack's Carrot Kugel

Yield: *10 servings*

16-ounce bag baby carrots

¹/₂ cup unsweetened
applesauce

¹/₄ cup granulated brown sugar

1 tablespoon ground cinnamon

1 teaspoon ground nutmeg

1 medium egg white

¹/₂ cup unsweetened pineapple
juice

1¹/₂ cups unbleached
all-purpose flour

1 teaspoon baking soda

1 teaspoon baking powder

Packaged baby carrots are so small they can be added to the food processor whole. For this recipe, use a 9-inch pie plate, or a shallow baking dish with a 1-inch-high rim.

1. Preheat the oven to 350°F. Spray a 9-inch pie plate with olive oil cooking spray and set aside.

2. Place the carrots in a food processor or blender, and finely chop. Transfer to a large bowl and add the applesauce, brown sugar, cinnamon, nutmeg, egg white, and pineapple juice. Blend well. Add the flour, baking soda, and baking powder. Mix well and spoon into the baking dish.

3. Bake for 1 hour, or until the kugel is set and the edges just begin to turn brown.

4. Allow to sit for 10 minutes before cutting into wedges and serving.

NUTRITIONAL FACTS (PER SERVING)
Calories: 109   Carbohydrates: 24.2 g   Cholesterol: 0 mg
Fat: 0.7 g   Fiber: 2.8 g   Protein: 3.3 g   Sodium: 186 mg

Miriam's Winter Squash Kugel

My friend Miriam claims her winter squash kugel is just as delicious as her husband Jack's carrot kugel (page 160). I agree. They're both sensational.

1. Preheat the oven to 350°F. Coat a 9-x-13-inch baking dish with olive oil cooking spray and set aside.

2. Place the squash in a microwave-safe bowl, cover with wax paper, and microwave for 7 minutes on High, or until the squash is just tender. Add to a blender or food processor and purée until smooth.

3. Combine the flour and brown sugar in a large bowl. Add the applesauce and egg whites, stirring until well-blended. Stir in the squash. Spoon mixture into the baking dish, then sprinkle with cinnamon, nutmeg, and allspice. Spoon orange juice evenly on top.

4. Bake for 40 minutes, or until the edges begin to brown.

5. Allow to cool 10 minutes before cutting into squares and serving.

Yield: *10 servings*

1 1/2 cups peeled, sliced fresh winter squash*

1 cup whole wheat flour

1/4 cup granulated brown sugar

2 tablespoons unsweetened applesauce

3 medium egg whites

1/4 teaspoon ground cinnamon

1/4 teaspoon ground nutmeg

1/8 teaspoon ground allspice

1/4 cup orange juice

* Can use 12-ounce package frozen, thawed squash. Can skip Step 2 and add squash directly to Step 3.

NUTRITIONAL FACTS (PER SERVING)
Calories: 73   Carbohydrates: 15.3 g   Cholesterol: 0 mg
Fat: 0.2 g   Fiber: 0.3 g   Protein: 2.6 g   Sodium: 19 mg

Creamy Yellow Squash Kugel

Yield: 10 servings

1 1/2 cups sliced yellow squash*

1 cup whole wheat flour

1/4 cup granulated brown sugar

1/4 cup skim milk

2 tablespoons unsweetened applesauce

3 medium egg whites

* Can use 12-ounce package frozen squash. Microwave for 4 minutes on High to cook, then drain.

When preparing this kugel to serve with meat dishes, substitute the milk with 1/8 cup light nondairy creamer mixed with 1/8 cup water.

1. Preheat the oven to 350°F. Coat a 9-x-13-inch baking dish with olive oil cooking spray and set aside.

2. Place the squash in a microwave-safe bowl, cover with wax paper, and microwave for 7 minutes on High, or until the squash is just tender.

3. Combine the flour and brown sugar in a large bowl. Add the milk, applesauce, and egg whites, stirring until well-blended. Stir in the squash. Spoon the mixture into the baking dish.

4. Bake for 1 hour, or until the edges begin to brown.

5. Allow to cool 10 minutes before cutting into squares and serving.

NUTRITIONAL FACTS (PER SERVING)
Calories: 67   Carbohydrates: 14.4 g   Cholesterol: 0 mg
Fat: 0.3 g   Fiber: 1.9 g   Protein: 3.1 g   Sodium: 22 mg

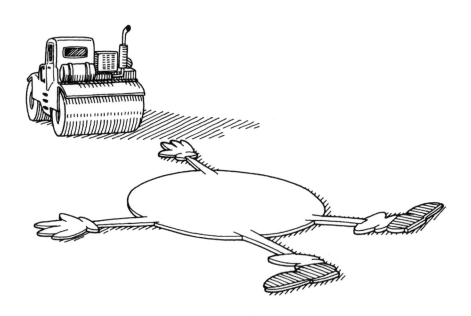

Evelyn's Cranberry-Pineapple Kugel

You can serve this sweet kugel as both a side dish or a dessert. It is delicious hot or cold.

1. Preheat the oven to 350°F. Coat a 9-x-13-inch baking dish with cooking spray and set aside.

2. Combine the flour, oats, brown sugar, and cinnamon in a medium bowl. Add the applesauce and mix to form fine crumbs.

3. Press half the crumb mixture into the baking dish. Layer the apples, cranberries, and pineapple on top. Cover with the remaining crumb mixture.

4. Bake for 1 hour, or until the top is brown.

5. Allow to cool 10 minutes before cutting into squares and serving.

Yield: *10 servings*

1 cup unbleached all-purpose flour

1 cup oat bran

2/3 cup granulated brown sugar

1 teaspoon ground cinnamon

3 tablespoons unsweetened applesauce

4 large apples, peeled and diced

16-ounce can whole cranberries

20-ounce can crushed pineapple, drained

NUTRITIONAL FACTS (PER SERVING)
Calories: 190   Carbohydrates: 47.8 g   Cholesterol: 0 mg
Fat: 1.3 g   Fiber: 6.8 g   Protein: 4 g   Sodium: 6 mg

Fruit Kugel

Yield: 10 servings

12 ounces "no yolk" egg noodles

1/2 cup raisins

1/2 cup pitted prunes

1/2 cup dried apricot halves

2 tablespoons unsweetened applesauce

2 medium apples peeled, cored, and diced

3 medium egg whites

1/4 teaspoon ground black pepper

1/2 teaspoon ground cinnamon

1 teaspoon granulated brown sugar

"No-yolk" egg noodles take the guilt out of noodle kugels. Enjoy this sweet fruit kugel hot or cold.

1. Preheat the oven to 350°F. Coat a 9-x-13-inch baking dish with cooking spray and set aside.

2. Bring 6 cups of water to boil in a medium saucepan. Add the noodles and cook according to package directions.

3. While the noodles are cooking, place the raisins, prunes, and apricots in a microwave-safe bowl and cover with water. Cover the bowl with wax paper and microwave for 2 minutes on High. Drain.

4. Combine the noodles, applesauce, apples, prunes, apricots, and raisins in a large bowl. Add the egg whites and black pepper, and mix well. Spoon the mixture into the baking dish, and sprinkle with cinnamon and brown sugar.

5. Bake for 45 minutes, or until the top is lightly brown.

6. Allow to cool 10 minutes before cutting into squares and serving.

NUTRITIONAL FACTS (PER SERVING)

Calories: 209   Carbohydrates: 43.3 g   Cholesterol: 0 mg
Fat: 0.5 g   Fiber: 3.4 g   Protein: 7.3 g   Sodium: 41 mg

Traditional Tsimmes

A very sweet traditional side dish.

Yield: *8 servings*

1. Preheat the oven to 350°F. Coat a medium baking dish with vegetable cooking spray and set aside.

2. Place the prunes in a microwave-safe bowl and cover with water. Cover the bowl with wax paper and microwave for 2 minutes on High. Drain.

3. Gently combine the sweet potatoes and honey in a large bowl. Add the carrots and prunes and mix gently. Spoon into the baking dish.

4. Bake uncovered for 1 hour or until the sweet potatoes are lightly brown.

5. Serve immediately.

1 cup pitted prunes

2 cups canned sweet potatoes, drained

1 tablespoon honey

3 medium carrots, peeled and cut into 1/2-inch slices

NUTRITIONAL FACTS (PER SERVING)
Calories: 109   Carbohydrates: 26.9 g   Cholesterol: 0 mg
Fat: 0.3 g   Fiber: 3.6 g   Protein: 1.6 g   Sodium: 37 g

"Don't Make a Big Tsimmes Out of It."

Tsimmes, a traditional side dish of slightly sweetened, mixed cooked fruits and vegetables, is derived from the German words zum (to the) and essen (eating). Since slow-cooked tsimmes has a lengthy baking time and is often mixed as it cooks, the word "tsimmes" has taken on new meanings over the years.

Today, the word tsimmes has come to mean a prolonged procedure, an involved business, or a mix-up, resulting in such expressions as:

- *"Don't make a big tsimmes out of it." (Don't make a federal case out of it.)*
- *"It's no tsimmes to me." (It's no big deal; it doesn't bother me.)*
- *"What a mess. It was a regular tsimmes." (A real mix-up; a mess; confusion.)*

Dried Fruit Tsimmes

Yield: *10 servings*

1 cup dried apricot halves

1 cup dried pear halves

1 cup pitted prunes

$1/2$ cup dark raisins

$1/2$ cup golden raisins

1 cup canned sweet potatoes, drained

1 tablespoon honey

The microwave helps make softening the dried fruit a snap. And don't limit yourself to the dried fruits called for in the ingredient list. Use the dried fruits of your choice in any combination.

1. Preheat the oven to 350°F. Coat a 9-x-13-inch baking dish with cooking spray and set aside.

2. Place the apricots, pears, prunes, and raisins in a microwave-safe bowl and cover with water. Cover the bowl with wax paper and microwave for 2 minutes on High, or until the fruit is soft but not mushy. Drain.

3. Cut the sweet potatoes in half and place in a large bowl. Add the honey, apricots, pears, prunes, and raisins, and mix gently. Spoon into the baking dish.

4. Bake for 1 hour, or until the sweet potatoes are lightly brown.

5. Serve immediately.

NUTRITIONAL FACTS (PER SERVING)
Calories: 146   Carbohydrates: 38.1 g   Cholesterol: 0 mg
Fat: 0.3 g   Fiber: 3.7 g   Protein: 1.6 g   Sodium: 15 mg

Homemade Cranberry Sauce

I enjoy making my own cranberry sauce. It contains half the sugar of most commercial varieties, and takes only 15 minutes to prepare. I usually keep a bag of cranberries in the freezer, where they keep for up to six months.

Yield: *2¹/₂ cups*

1 cup water

¹/₂ cup sugar

12-ounce bag fresh cranberries

1. Bring the water to a boil in a small saucepan. Add the sugar and stir until dissolved.

2. Add the cranberries and return to a boil. Cook uncovered for 5 minutes, stirring occasionally. Reduce the heat to low and simmer uncovered for 10 minutes.

3. Transfer the cranberries to a bowl, cover, and refrigerate until chilled.

NUTRITIONAL FACTS (PER ¹/₄-CUP SERVING)
Calories: 55   Carbohydrates: 14.1 g   Cholesterol: 0 mg
Fat: 0.1 g   Fiber: 1.4 g   Protein: 0.1 g   Sodium: 1 mg

Zucchini, Tomato, & Potato Casserole

Yield: *8 servings*

2 medium zucchini, cut into
1-inch slices

2 medium tomatoes, cut into
1-inch slices

2 medium potatoes, cut into
1-inch slices

10 fresh basil leaves, or 2¹/₂
tablespoons dried

1 teaspoon olive oil

¹/₄ teaspoon ground black
pepper

This delicious blend of vegetables goes well with a wide variety of dishes.

1. Preheat the oven to 350°F. Coat a 9-x-13-inch baking dish with olive oil cooking spray.

2. Layer the zucchini in the bottom of the baking dish. Top with a layer of potatoes, and follow with a layer of tomatoes.

3. Toss the basil leaves with olive oil, and place them on top of the casserole. Sprinkle with black pepper.

4. Bake covered for 1 hour, or until the edges of the casserole begin to brown.

5. Cut into squares and serve hot or cold.

NUTRITIONAL FACTS (PER SERVING)

Calories: 32   Carbohydrates: 6 g   Cholesterol: 0 mg
Fat: 0.7 g   Fiber: 1 g   Protein: 1.1 g   Sodium: 5 mg

Latkes (Potato Pancakes)

Traditionally eaten on the holiday of Chanukah, these delicious latkes are cooked in a nonstick skillet that has been coated with olive oil cooking spray.

1. Add alternating chunks of potatoes and onion to a food processor and process until smooth. Transfer this mixture to a fine mesh strainer to drain the excess liquid, then place in a large bowl. Add the remaining ingredients, mix well, and allow to stand for 5 minutes.

2. Spray a large nonstick skillet with cooking spray and place over medium heat until the oil is hot but not smoking. Drop heaping tablespoons of the potato mixture into the skillet and flatten with the back of the spoon. Cook about 2 minutes on each side or until lightly brown.

3. Place the latkes on a serving platter and allow to cool 5 minutes before serving. Delicious when accompanied by unsweetened applesauce.

Yield: *30 latkes*

7 medium baked potatoes, peeled and cut into chunks

1 large onion, cut into chunks

4 medium egg whites

1/4 cup unsalted matzoh meal

1/8 teaspoon ground white pepper

NUTRITIONAL FACTS (PER LATKE)
Calories: 28   Carbohydrates: 5.9 g   Cholesterol: 0 mg
Fat: 0.1 g   Fiber: 0.5 g   Protein: 1.2 g   Sodium: 27 mg

When Cooking Vegetables

Keep the following helpful tips in mind when cooking vegetables:

- *As most of a vegetable's nutrients are concentrated just under its skin, avoid peeling whenever possible.*
- *When precooked vegetables are needed in a recipe, use the microwave for minimum fuss and quick cooking time.*
- *To preserve their nutrients, steam vegetables in the microwave or on the stovetop.*
- *Try to choose nutrient-rich fresh vegetables over frozen and canned varieties whenever possible.*

Mushroom Rice

Yield: *6 servings*

1 cup brown rice

2 cups water

1 cup sliced mushrooms

2 tablespoons chopped fresh
thyme

2 tablespoons chopped fresh
rosemary

A simple side dish with a light herb flavor.

1. Bring the water to boil in a medium saucepan. Add the rice, reduce the heat to low, and simmer covered for 30 minutes.

2. Stir in the mushrooms, thyme, and rosemary, and simmer another 5 minutes, or until the rice is tender and flakes with a fork.

3. Place in a serving bowl and enjoy hot.

NUTRITIONAL FACTS (PER SERVING)
Calories: 128   Carbohydrates: 27.4 g   Cholesterol: 0 mg
Fat: 1.1 g   Fiber: 0.6 g   Protein: 3.2 g   Sodium: 6 mg

VARIATION

- To reduce the cooking time, use instant rice instead of the longer-cooking variety.

Asparagus au Naturel

Yield: *6 servings*

1 pound fresh asparagus
spears, trimmed

½ teaspoon chopped fresh
basil

1 tablespoon chopped garlic

This simple side dish can be ready in less than 10 minutes Try it topped with Yogurt-Dill Sauce (page 135) or Sweet Dill Sauce (page 136).

1. Place the asparagus spears in a microwave-safe baking dish. Sprinkle with basil and garlic. Cover the dish with wax paper and microwave for 4 minutes on High, or until the asparagus is tender.

2. Serve hot.

NUTRITIONAL FACTS (PER SERVING)
Calories: 12   Carbohydrates: 2.3 g   Cholesterol: 0 mg
Fat: 0.1 g   Fiber: 0.9 g   Protein: 1 g   Sodium: 1 mg

Spinach-Mushroom Medley

For a different taste, try adding a drop or two of balsamic vinegar to this dish before serving.

1. Place the olive oil, mushrooms, and garlic in a large skillet over medium-low heat. Stirring frequently, cook the mushrooms for 2 minutes or until soft.

2. Add the spinach and basil. Increase the heat to medium and cook for 7 to 8 minutes, or until the spinach is wilted.

3. Using a slotted spoon, transfer the mixture to a serving bowl. Enjoy hot.

Yield: *8 servings*

1 teaspoon olive oil

2 cups sliced Portabella mushrooms

1 garlic clove, finely chopped

2 1/2 cups fresh spinach leaves, washed thoroughly and patted dry*

1 tablespoon chopped fresh basil

* Can use 20-ounce package frozen spinach, thawed and drained. Cook for 3 to 4 minutes.

NUTRITIONAL FACTS (PER SERVING)
Calories: 22   Carbohydrates: 3 g   Cholesterol: 0 mg
Fat: 0.8 g   Fiber: 1.7 g   Protein: 1.9 g   Sodium: 41 mg

Steamed Broccoli with Tarragon

Just a hint of tarragon gives this dish its unique flavor.

1. Place the broccoli in a microwave steamer and add 1 tablespoon of water. Cover and steam for 3 minutes on High. Add the tarragon and onion, and steam another 2 minutes, or until the broccoli is just tender. If you do not have a steamer, cook the broccoli in a microwave-safe bowl that is covered with wax paper. You can also steam the broccoli in a pot on the stovetop.

2. Transfer to a serving bowl and enjoy immediately.

Yield: *6 servings*

1 pound fresh broccoli, cut into bite-sized pieces

1 tablespoon chopped fresh tarragon

1 tablespoon finely chopped onion

NUTRITIONAL FACTS (PER SERVING)
Calories: 22   Carbohydrates: 4.4 g   Cholesterol: 0 mg
Fat: 0.3 g   Fiber: 2.3 g   Protein: 2.3 g   Sodium: 27 mg

Sweet Sweet Potatoes

Yield: *8 servings*

4 medium sweet potatoes

1 tablespoon honey

1/2 teaspoon ground cinnamon

1/4 teaspoon ground allspice

Sweet potatoes are rich in vitamins A and C.

1. Preheat the oven to 350°F. Coat a 9-x-13-inch baking dish with olive oil cooking spray and set aside.

2. Scrub the sweet potatoes, cut them in half lengthwise, and place in the baking dish cut side up. Spoon the honey on top and sprinkle with cinnamon and allspice.

3. Bake uncovered for 20 minutes, then turn the potatoes over and continue to bake cut side down for another 20 minutes or until soft.

4. Serve the potatoes in their skins.

NUTRITIONAL FACTS (PER SERVING)
Calories: 58   Carbohydrates: 13.7 g   Cholesterol: 0 mg
Fat: 0.2 g   Fiber: 1.5 g   Protein: 0.8 g   Sodium: 6 mg

VARIATIONS

• To microwave, place the prepared potatoes in a microwave-safe bowl, cover with wax paper, and cook on High for 7 minutes, or until the potatoes are tender.

• For a different taste, try scooping the potatoes from their skins and mixing with canned pineapple chunks before serving.

Cauliflower and Mustard Sauce

Cauliflower is one of the cancer-preventive cruciferous vegetables. It is high in fiber and low in calories.

Yield: *6 servings*

1. Place the cauliflower in a microwave-safe baking dish. Add the water, cover with wax paper, and microwave for 7 minutes, or until the cauliflower is tender.

2. While the cauliflower is cooking, make a sauce by combining the mayonnaise and mustard.

3. Spoon the sauce over the hot cooked cauliflower and serve.

3 cups cauliflower florets

1 tablespoon water

2 tablespoons fat-free mayonnaise

1 tablespoon Dijon-style mustard

NUTRITIONAL FACTS (PER SERVING)
Calories: 18   Carbohydrates: 3.4 g   Cholesterol: 0 mg
Fat: 0.2 g   Fiber: 1.3 g   Protein: 1.1 g   Sodium: 88 mg

Cheddar Brussels Sprouts

One of the cruciferous vegetables, Brussels sprouts are delicious and easy to cook in this dairy dish.

Yield: *6 servings*

1. Place the Brussels sprouts in a microwave-safe baking dish and sprinkle with onion. Add the water, cover with wax paper, and microwave on high for 5 minutes, or until the sprouts are tender.

2. Spoon the cheddar spread over the Brussels sprouts and microwave another 10 seconds on High.

3. Serve hot or cold.

12 ounces fresh Brussels sprouts

2 tablespoons finely chopped onion

1 tablespoon water

1 tablespoon fat-free cheddar cheese spread

NUTRITIONAL FACTS (PER SERVING)
Calories: 24   Carbohydrates: 4.7 g   Cholesterol: 0 mg
Fat: 0.2 g   Fiber: 2.2 g   Protein: 2.1 g   Sodium: 34 mg

Kasha Varnishkes

Yield: *12 servings*

1 large onion, diced

1 cup kasha (buckwheat)

1 medium egg white

2 cups boiling water

1/4 teaspoon ground black
   pepper

6 ounces bow tie pasta

1 teaspoon olive oil

Try this delicious low-fat version of a traditional Old-World dish.

1. Coat a 2-quart saucepan with olive oil cooking spray and place over medium-low heat. Add the onion and sauté for 5 minutes or until light brown. Add the kasha and egg white and blend well. Cook for 2 minutes while stirring frequently.

2. Stir the boiling water into the saucepan, add the pepper, and mix well. Reduce the heat to low and simmer covered for 15 minutes or until the kasha has absorbed the liquid.

3. While the kasha is simmering, cook the pasta according to package directions. Drain well.

4. Place the kasha in a large serving bowl, add the pasta and olive oil, and mix well. Serve hot.

NUTRITIONAL FACTS (PER SERVING)
Calories: 108   Carbohydrates: 21.3 g   Cholesterol: 0 mg
Fat: 1.1 g   Fiber: 1.9 g   Protein: 4.1 g   Sodium: 51 mg

Sweet Spinach

When cooking frozen vegetables in the microwave, it's not necessary to add any water.

1. Place the spinach, onion, and basil in a microwave-safe baking dish. If using fresh spinach, add 1 tablespoon of water.

2. Cover the dish with wax paper and microwave for 7 minutes on High. (If using frozen spinach, microwave for 5 minutes.)

3. Spoon the salad dressing over the cooked spinach and serve hot.

Yield: 6 servings

1 1/2 cups chopped fresh spinach leaves, or 12-ounce package frozen

1 cup chopped Vidalia or other sweet onion

1 teaspoon chopped fresh basil

1 tablespoon fat-free French salad dressing

NUTRITIONAL FACTS (PER SERVING)

Calories: 15 Carbohydrates: 4.2 g Cholesterol: 0 mg
Fat: 0.2 g Fiber: 1.4 g Protein: 1.4 g Sodium: 148 mg

Spicy Corn Mix

This vibrant blend of colorful ingredients adds visual appeal to any dish.

1. Place all of the ingredients in a microwave-safe baking dish. If using fresh corn, add 1 tablespoon of water.

2. Cover the dish and microwave for 5 minutes on High, or until the vegetables are tender.

3. Toss the ingredients together and serve.

Yield: 8 servings

2 cups fresh or frozen corn kernels

2 cups fresh or frozen red bell pepper slices

2 drops hot pepper sauce

1/4 teaspoon crushed red pepper flakes

NUTRITIONAL FACTS (PER SERVING)

Calories: 43 Carbohydrates: 10.1 g Cholesterol: 0 mg
Fat: 0.4 g Fiber: 1.6 g Protein: 1.5 g Sodium: 2 mg

Baked Portabella Mushrooms

Yield: *6 servings*

1 pound Portabella mushrooms, cut into 1-inch-thick slices

¼ teaspoon olive oil

1 tablespoon chopped fresh basil

Portabella mushrooms have a wonderful rich flavor and meaty texture.

1. Preheat the oven to 350°F. Coat a medium baking dish with olive oil cooking spray.

2. Place the mushrooms in the baking dish and sprinkle with basil. Drizzle the olive oil on top.

3. Bake covered for 10 minutes, or until the mushrooms are soft and tender.

4. Serve hot.

NUTRITIONAL FACTS (PER SERVING)
Calories: 22   Carbohydrates: 3.9 g   Cholesterol: 0 mg
Fat: 0.5 g   Fiber: 1 g   Protein: 1.6 g   Sodium: 3 mg

Lima Beans with Tarragon

Yield: *6 servings*

8 ounces linguine

2 cups cooked lima beans*

1 teaspoon chopped fresh garlic

1 tablespoon chopped fresh tarragon, or 1 teaspoon dried

¼ teaspoon olive oil

* Can use 16-ounce package frozen lima beans. Place in a microwave-safe bowl, cover, and cook for 4 minutes on High. Drain before adding to recipe.

Serve this tasty pasta dish as a side dish or entrée.

1. Bring 6 cups of water to boil in a medium saucepan. Add the linguine and cook according to package directions.

2. While the linguine is cooking, heat the beans in a small saucepan over medium-low heat. Add the tarragon, garlic, and olive oil. Mix well.

3. Place the cooked linguine in a large bowl, add the bean mixture, and mix well.

4. Serve hot.

NUTRITIONAL FACTS (PER SERVING)
Calories: 163   Carbohydrates: 31.4 g   Cholesterol: 0 mg
Fat: 0.8 g   Fiber: 4 g   Protein: 7.4 g   Sodium: 3 mg

Potluck Rice and Beans

I call this dish "potluck" because I make it with whatever soup or broth I have on hand.

1. Combine all of the ingredients in a medium saucepan. Simmer over low heat for 10 minutes, or until the mushrooms are soft and the ingredients are heated through.

2. Spoon into a serving bowl and enjoy hot.

Yield: *8 servings*

2 cups cooked red kidney beans, rinsed and drained

2 cups cooked brown rice

1 cup sliced mushrooms

1 tablespoon dried savory

2 tablespoons low-sodium soup or broth (any variety)

NUTRITIONAL FACTS (PER SERVING)
Calories: 115   Fat: 0.7 g   Protein: 5.3 g   Cholesterol: 0 mg
Fiber: 3.4 g   Sodium: 6 mg   Carbohydrates: 22.3 g

Tangy Rice and Beans

This dish gets its zing from sweet-and-sour sauce, which is low in calories and fat-free.

1. Combine all of the ingredients in a medium saucepan. Simmer over low heat for 10 minutes, or until the ingredients are heated through.

2. Spoon into a serving bowl and enjoy hot.

Yield: *8 servings*

2 cups cooked pinto beans

1 cup cooked brown rice

2 tablespoons sweet-and-sour sauce, or Chinese duck sauce

NUTRITIONAL FACTS (PER SERVING)
Calories: 149   Fat: 0.9 g   Protein: 5.3 g   Cholesterol: 0 mg
Fiber: 3.7 g   Sodium: 14 mg   Carbohydrates: 30.2 g

Beans with Fajita Sauce

Yield: *8 servings*

2 cups vegetarian bean mix, rinsed and drained

1 medium sweet onion, finely chopped

6 medium baking potatoes

2 tablespoons fajita sauce

Mexican-style fajita sauce is one of the latest kosher-certified products to make its way to supermarket shelves. As an added bonus, it is fat-free with very few calories.

1. Wash the potatoes, pierce them several times with a fork or knife, and place them in a microwave-safe baking dish. Cover with wax paper and cook 7 minutes on High, or until the potatoes are tender.

2. Combine the beans, onion, and fajita sauce in a medium saucepan. When the potatoes are cool enough to handle, cut them into 2-inch chunks and add to the beans. Mix well.

3. Cook over medium-low heat for 10 minutes, or until the onions are soft and the ingredients are heated through.

4. Spoon into a serving bowl and enjoy immediately.

NUTRITIONAL FACTS (PER SERVING)

Calories: 115   Carbohydrates: 23.3 g   Cholesterol: 0 mg
Fat: 0.4 g   Fiber: 5.3 g   Protein: 5.5 g   Sodium: 39 mg

Beans in the Crockpot

Try this delicious hearty blend of beans as a side dish or as a topping for rice or pasta.

1. Place the chick peas, kidney beans, onion, and garlic in a 3-quart crockpot. Add enough water to just cover the ingredients. Crumble the bouillon and add it to the pot along with the basil.

2. Cook for 2 to 3 hours on Low. (If using dried beans, cook for 8 to 10 hours, or until the beans are soft.)

3. Ladle into bowls and serve hot.

NUTRITIONAL FACTS (PER SERVING)

Calories: 175   Carbohydrates: 32.1 g   Cholesterol: 0 mg

Fat: 0.7 g   Fiber: 10.5 g   Protein: 11.6 g   Sodium: 118 mg

---

Yield: *8 Servings*

16-ounce can chick peas, undrained*

16-ounce can red kidney beans, undrained*

1 large Vidalia or other sweet onion, thickly sliced

2 garlic cloves

1 beef bouillon cube

2 tablespoons fresh basil leaves

* Can use 1 cup dried beans for each 16-ounce can. (*See* inset on page 29 for presoaking instructions.)

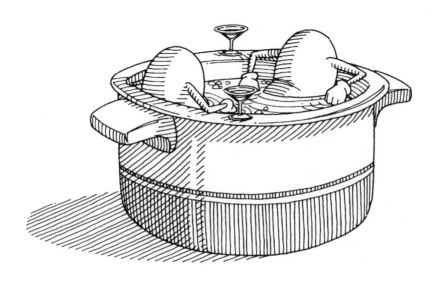

Campfire Beans

Yield: *6 servings*

16-ounce can navy beans, rinsed and drained*

1 large sweet onion, coarsely chopped

2 garlic cloves, sliced

1/4 cup molasses

1/4 cup Dijon-style mustard

1 teaspoon paprika

4 cloves

1/2 cinnamon stick

1 bay leaf

* Can use 1 cup dried beans. (*See* inset on page 29 for presoaking instructions.)

A delicious slow-cooked bean dish.

1. Add the navy beans, onion, garlic, molasses, mustard, and paprika to a 3-quart crockpot. Place the cloves, cinnamon, and bay leaf on top of the mixture. Add just enough water to cover.

2. Cook for 2 to 3 hours on Low. (If using dried beans, cook for 8 to 10 hours, or until the beans are soft.)

3. Ladle into bowls and serve hot.

NUTRITIONAL FACTS (PER SERVING)
Calories: 128   Carbohydrates: 25 g   Cholesterol: 0 mg
Fat: 0.7 g   Fiber: 7.1 g   Protein: 6.6 g   Sodium: 104 mg

Grandma Helen's Hungarian Noodles with Cabbage

An authentic Hungarian side dish.

Yield: *10 servings*

1. Bring a large pot of water to a boil. Add the linguine and cook according to package directions.

2. While the water is coming to a boil, combine the cabbage and olive oil in a nonstick skillet over medium heat. Cook uncovered for 8 to 10 minutes stirring frequently, or until the cabbage is soft and beginning to brown. Add the black pepper and mix well.

3. Place the cooked pasta in a large bowl. Add the cabbage mixture and toss together.

4. Serve hot.

1 pound linguine, fettuccine, or other long, flat pasta

1 1/2 cups shredded cabbage*

1 teaspoon olive oil

1/2 teaspoon ground black pepper

* Can use 12-ounce package frozen cabbage, thawed and drained.

NUTRITIONAL FACTS (PER SERVING)

Calories: 175   Carbohydrates: 34.5 g   Cholesterol: 0 mg
Fat: 1.2 g   Fiber: 1.1 g   Protein: 5.9 g   Sodium: 5 mg

Time-Saving Tip

Need to prepare a dish that calls for fresh vegetables, but don't have the time to cook them? Frozen vegetables, while not as desirable as fresh, are an acceptable substitute in most dishes. Always keep a few varieties on hand in your freezer.

Karen's Tabbouleh

Yield: *8 servings*

8 ounces medium-ground
   bulghur wheat

2 medium scallions, light green
   and white part only, coarsely
   chopped

3 medium plum tomatoes,
   chopped

1 tablespoon chopped fresh
   mint

1 tablespoon vinegar

1 teaspoon olive oil

This is a wonderful Sephardic dish.

1. Place the bulghur in a large bowl and cover with cold water. Soak for 3 hours (adding water as needed to keep the wheat covered), or until the wheat is soft yet somewhat chewy.

2. Drain the wheat well, and place in a bowl along with the scallions, tomatoes, mint, olive oil, and vinegar. Mix well.

3. Cover and refrigerate for 1 hour or until chilled.

4. Store any leftover tabbouleh in a sealed container in the refrigerator for up to one week.

NUTRITIONAL FACTS (PER SERVING)
Calories: 113   Carbohydrates: 24 g   Cholesterol: 0 mg
Fat: 1.1 g   Fiber: 5.8 g   Protein: 3.9 g   Sodium: 43 mg

Tomato Pasta Salad

Yield: *8 servings*

2 cups bowties, shells, or other
   small pasta (spinach-flavored)

1 cup chopped tomatoes

2 cups vegetarian bean mix,
   rinsed and drained

1 cup sliced green beans

1/4 teaspoon lemon juice

1 large sweet onion, finely
   chopped

A refreshing cold pasta salad.

1. Bring 6 cups of water to boil in a medium saucepan. Add the pasta and cook according to package directions.

2. While the pasta is cooking, combine the remaining ingredients in a large bowl.

3. Add the cooked pasta to the bowl and mix the ingredients well. Cover and refrigerate for 30 minutes, or until chilled.

NUTRITIONAL FACTS (PER SERVING)
Calories: 178   Carbohydrates: 36.2 g   Cholesterol: 0 mg
Fat: 0.8 g   Fiber: 9.5 g   Protein: 9.2 g   Sodium: 86 mg

Top Left: Karen's Tabbouleh (page 182)
Top Right: Curried Chicken (page 112)
Bottom: Turkish Meat Pie (page 146)

Top Left: Challah (page 184)

Top Right: Sweet Sweet Potatoes
(page 172)

Center Left: Mushroom Rice (page 170)

Bottom Right: Apricot Turkey Roast
(page 138) with Homemade Cranberry
Sauce (page 167)

Party-Colored Pasta Salad

Use both spinach and carrot pasta for added color.

Yield: *8 servings*

1. Bring 6 cups of water to boil in a medium saucepan. Add the pasta and cook according to package directions.

2. While the pasta is cooking, combine the remaining ingredients in a large bowl.

3. Add the cooked pasta to the bowl and mix the ingredients well. Cover and refrigerate for 30 minutes, or until chilled.

2 cups radiatorre, springs, or other curly-shaped pasta (spinach- and/or carrot-flavored)

16-ounce can red kidney beans, rinsed and drained

1 medium red bell pepper, seeded and finely chopped

1 tablespoon chopped fresh basil

1 tablespoon Dijon-style mustard

1 tablespoon fat-free mayonnaise

NUTRITIONAL FACTS (PER SERVING)
Calories: 163   Carbohydrates: 33.8 g   Cholesterol: 0 mg
Fat: 0.7 g   Fiber: 6.1 g   Protein: 8.3 g   Sodium: 53 mg

Simply Chilled Pasta Salad

This quick and easy pasta salad is perfect fare for a summer afternoon.

Yield: *8 servings*

1. Bring 6 cups of water to boil in a medium saucepan. Add the pasta and cook according to package directions. Drain.

2. Transfer the cooked pasta to a large bowl along with the remaining ingredients. Toss together well.

3. Refrigerate at least 30 minutes before serving.

2 cups shells or other small pasta

16-ounce can chick peas, undrained

1 cup corn kernels

1 tablespoon chopped fresh basil

1/2 teaspoon olive oil

NUTRITIONAL FACTS (PER SERVING)
Calories: 187   Carbohydrates: 37 g   Cholesterol: 0 mg
Fat: 1.5 g   Fiber: 3.7 g   Protein: 6.9 g   Sodium: 172 mg

Challah

The traditional bread eaten on the Sabbath and holidays, challah is typically made with oil and eggs. This fat-free challah will pleasantly surprise those who think challah that tastes good has to be high in fat and calories. Like most yeasted breads, this recipe may be bit time consuming, but the effort is certainly worth it.

Yield: *2 large loaves*

2 packages active dry yeast
  ($1/4$-ounce each)

$1^1/2$ cups warm water

$1/2$ cup granulated sugar

$6^1/2$ cups unbleached all-
  purpose flour

$1/4$ cup pear baby food

4 medium egg whites

GLAZE

1 medium egg white, beaten

1. Combine the yeast, $1/2$ cup of the warm water, and 1 teaspoon of the sugar in a small bowl and let it stand until foamy (about 5 minutes).* If the water does not foam, discard it and begin again with fresh yeast.

2. Using an electric mixer or food processor with dough blade attachments, combine 4 cups of the flour with the remaining pears and sugar to form coarse crumbs. Add the yeast mixture, remaining water, and egg whites. Beat for 3 minutes, then add the remaining flour, $1/2$ cup at a time, to form a soft, slightly sticky dough. Cover with plastic wrap and let rest 10 minutes.

3. Knead the dough by hand until smooth, or divide in half and knead in a food processor. Form the dough into a ball and place in a bowl that has been lightly coated with cooking spray. Roll the dough over to coat all sides. Cover with plastic wrap and a clean dish towel, and let stand in a warm place for 1 hour or until the dough has doubled in size.

4. Using a floured fist, punch down the dough, then turn it onto a floured board. Divide the dough in half, then divide each half in thirds. Cover loosely with plastic wrap and let rest 10 minutes.

5. Roll out each piece of dough into 12-inch long strands that are 1 inch in diameter. On a baking sheet that has been coated with cooking spray, braid 3 strands as pictured on the next page. On a separate baking sheet, braid the remaining 3 strands.

6. Lightly spray each loaf with cooking spray to prevent the dough from drying out. Cover with wax paper and let rise for 1 hour or until doubled in size.

7. Preheat the oven to 375°F. Brush the loaves with beaten egg white, then bake for 40 to 45 minutes or until the loaves are brown.

8. Allow to cool 30 minutes before serving.

* Be sure to use warm water only when checking (proofing) the yeast. If the water is too hot, it will kill the yeast. If the water is too cold, the yeast will work too slowly.

VARIATION

• To make round challahs, after dividing the dough in half and allowing to rest 10 minutes, roll each half into 18-inch-long strands that are 2 inches in diameter. Place the end of a strand in the middle of a baking sheet, then coil the strand around itself. (*See* Forming Challah on next page.)

NUTRITIONAL FACTS (PER $1/2$-INCH SLICE)
Calories: 68   Carbohydrates: 14.1 g   Cholesterol: 0 mg
Fat: 0.2 g   Fiber: 0.3 g   Protein: 2.1 g   Sodium: 6 mg

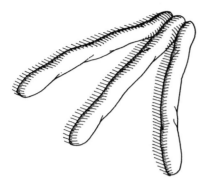

1. *Place the ends of three strands together.*

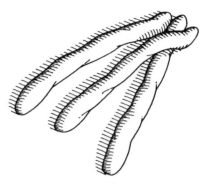

2. *Bring the right strand over the middle one.*

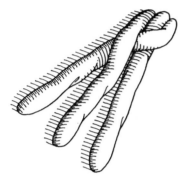

3. *Bring the left strand over the middle strand.*

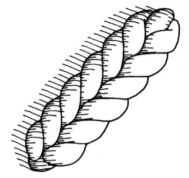

4. *Repeat until the strands are braided.*

A Braided Challah

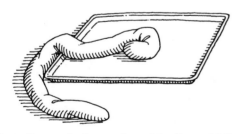

1. *Place the end of one strand in the middle of a baking sheet.*

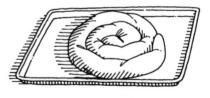

2. *Coil the strand around itself.*

A Round Challah

Forming Challah

9.
Desserts

One might think it is impossible to fit delicious desserts into a low-fat, low-calorie lifestyle. Not true. For one thing, desserts can be healthful by nature. Always think "fruit." With its natural sweetness and refreshing nature, fruit can be the perfect snack or delicious ending to any meal. Try an unadorned bowl of colorful mixed fruit salad or a dish of sliced melon topped with a scoop of fruit sorbet. A simple plate of fresh berries crowned with a dab of fat-free whipped topping is another good choice. When using whipped toppings, however, be sure to read labels. Some fat-free toppings are dairy even though their low-fat or regular counterparts may be pareve.

What about baked goods? A few ingredient substitutions can turn a number of tradition-ally high-fat choices into low-fat creations. The key is making the right substitutions for the high-fat ingredients. For instance, in most baked items I use fruit purées instead of oil or shortening. Unsweetened applesauce is one of my favorites. I always keep small 4-ounce

containers on hand. They're convenient, readily available, and may be stored unrefrig-erated before opening. They also come in a variety of lively flavors—raspberry, cranberry, tropical fruit, and strawberry, to name a few. The added flavor enhances the taste of muffins and cakes. For example, to add fla-vor to my Cranberry Loaf, I use cranberry applesauce.

Apple butter, apricot butter, and many puréed baby foods are also good choices for oil substitutes. Delicately flavored pear baby food, for instance, has practically no taste and is suitable to use in pastries, as well as light cakes, such as sponge and angel food. Prune butter (lekvar) is the best fat substitute for providing moisture and texture to baked goods. However, because of its dark color, I use it only for chocolate cakes, chocloate chip cookies, honey cakes, and other "dark-colored" baked goods.

When replacing the fat in a recipe with fruit butter or fruit purée, use the following formula:

| 1 cup butter or margarine | = | ½ cup fruit purée or fruit butter |
| 1 cup oil or other liquid shortening | = | ¾ cup fruit purée or fruit butter |

You'll enjoy the desserts in this chapter. Choose from a number of fresh fruit creations, such as Farm Fresh Applesauce, Ripe Peach Compote, and Kiwi Parfait, or try one of the baked items like Chewy Chocolate Chip Cookies, Easy-Bake Hamantaschen, and Rosh Hashanah Honey Cake. One thing is sure, all of the desserts are tasty and delicious with practically no fat and very few calories. Enjoy.

Apple Butter

Yield: *2 cups*

6 medium apples, peeled, cored, and sliced (Macintosh, Cortland, Rome Beauty, or combination of)

½ cup granulated sugar

½ cup dark brown sugar, packed

½ teaspoon ground cinnamon

⅛ teaspoon ground nutmeg

3 allspice berries

3 cloves

Creamy smooth apple butter makes a delicious topping for muffins, rolls, and bagels.

1. Combine all of the ingredients in a microwave-safe bowl. Cover tightly with plastic wrap and microwave for 15 minutes on High, or until the apples are soft.

2. Carefully remove the plastic wrap. (To prevent the steam from burning your hands and face, peel back the plastic wrap from the side of the bowl that is farthest from you.)

3. Remove and discard the cloves and allspice berries, then transfer the remaining ingredients to a food processor or blender and process until smooth. Return the mixture to the bowl and microwave uncovered for 10 minutes on High.

4. Use warm or cold on fat-free muffins, rolls, or bagels.

NUTRITIONAL FACTS (PER TABLESPOON)
Calories: 40   Carbohydrates: 10.4 g   Cholesterol: 0 mg
Fat: 0.1 g   Fiber: 0.9 g   Protein: 0.1 g   Sodium: 0 mg

Farm Fresh Applesauce

Feel free to use or combine any number of apple varieties when making this tasty applesauce.

1. Combine all of the ingredients in a large pot over very low heat. Simmer partially covered, stirring occasionally, for 45 minutes, or until the apples are soft.

2. Remove and discard the allspice berries and cloves, then transfer the applesauce to a bowl. Refrigerate at least 30 minutes.

3. Serve chilled.

Yield: *8 cups*

8 large apples, peeled, cored, and sliced (Macintosh, Cortland, Rome Beauty, or combination of)

2 cups water

1/4 cup granulated brown sugar

1/2 teaspoon ground cinnamon

3 allspice berries

3 cloves

NUTRITIONAL FACTS (PER 1/2-CUP SERVING)

Calories: 46   Carbohydrates: 11.9 g   Cholesterol: 0 mg
Fat: 0.2 g   Fiber: 1.8 g   Protein: 0.1 g   Sodium: 2 mg

My Mother's Favorite Microwave-Baked Apples

Yield: *6 servings*

6 medium Cortland or Rome Beauty apples, washed and cored

6 tablespoons water

1½ teaspoons ground cinnamon

Simple and easy to prepare, these baked apples are a favorite treat on a chilly autumn day.

1. Using a fork, poke holes in the outside of each apple, then stand them up in a microwave-safe baking dish.

2. Place ¼ teaspoon of cinnamon in the cored center of each apple, followed by a tablespoon of water.

3. Cover with wax paper and microwave for 12 to 18 minutes on High (about 2 to 3 minutes of cooking time per apple).

4. Serve hot or chilled.

NUTRITIONAL FACTS (PER SERVING)

Calories: 76   Carbohydrates: 19.8 g   Cholesterol: 0 mg
Fat: 0.5 g   Fiber: 3.7 g   Protein: 0.3 g   Sodium: 1 mg

VARIATIONS

- For extra sweetness, add a little granulated brown sugar or honey to the apples before baking.
- Use Granny Smith apples for a tangier taste.

My Father's Microwave Applesauce

Cooking time and sweetener amount will vary somewhat according to the type of apples used. Store any leftover applesauce in sealed plastic containers in the freezer.

Yield: *8 cups*

8 large apples of any variety (try to include at least 1 Granny Smith), peeled, cored, and cut into 1-inch chunks

1/2 cup water

1/4 cup granulated sugar

1. Place the apples and water in a microwave-safe bowl. Cover with wax paper and microwave for 16 minutes on High, or until the apples are soft.

2. Remove the apples from the microwave and crush with a fork until somewhat smooth. Cover, return to the microwave, and cook another 8 minutes.

3. Continue to crush the apples until smooth. Add the sugar and mix well. Cover and refrigerate.

4. Serve chilled.

NUTRITIONAL FACTS (PER 1/2-CUP SERVING)

Calories: 44   Carbohydrates: 11.2 g   Cholesterol: 0 mg

Fat: 0.2 g   Fiber: 1.7 g   Protein: 0.1 g   Sodium: 0 mg

Blueberry Parfait

Yield: *8 servings*

1 quart ripe blueberries (4 cups)

1 cup sweet white dessert wine

2 tablespoons granulated brown sugar

2 cups nonfat vanilla yogurt

A colorful, refreshing dairy dessert.

1. Place the blueberries, wine, and sugar in a blender or food processor and purée about 10 seconds. Cover and refrigerate for 30 minutes.

2. Pour the chilled blueberries into parfait glasses, top each with ¼ cup of yogurt, and serve.

NUTRITIONAL FACTS (PER SERVING)

Calories: 124   Carbohydrates: 21.1 g   Cholesterol: 1 mg
Fat: 0.4 g   Fiber: 1.9 g   Protein: 3.4 g   Sodium: 45 mg

VARIATION

• Try different fruits or combinations of fruits to create unusual flavors. For sweet fruits like cherries, apricots, or peaches, use 2 tablespoons sugar. For tangier fruits such as grapes, oranges, or grapefruits, use 3 to 5 tablespoons sugar.

Kiwi Parfait

This dairy dessert, with its vibrant green and creamy white colors, makes a beautiful presentation.

Yield: *8 servings*

1. Using your fingers, peel the ripe kiwi fruit, then cut each into 4 slices.

2. Place the kiwi, wine, and sugar in a blender or food processor, and purée about 10 seconds. Cover and refrigerate for 30 minutes.

3. Pour the chilled kiwi blend into parfait glasses, top each with ¼ cup of yogurt, and serve.

2 pounds ripe kiwi fruit

1 cup sweet white dessert wine

3 tablespoons granulated sugar

2 cups nonfat vanilla yogurt

NUTRITIONAL FACTS (PER SERVING)
Calories: 149   Carbohydrates: 26.7 g   Cholesterol: 1 mg
Fat: 0.5 g   Fiber: 3.3 g   Protein: 3.9 g   Sodium: 45 mg

Dried Fruit Compote

An easy-to-prepare dessert that you cook in the microwave.

Yield: *8 servings*

1. Place the apricots, pears, prunes, and peaches in a microwave-safe baking dish. Add the water and brown sugar and mix well.

2. Cover with wax paper and microwave for 10 minutes on High.

3. Remove from the microwave and allow to cool 5 to 10 minutes. Stir gently and refrigerate 30 to 60 minutes.

4. Spoon into bowls and serve.

1 cup dried apricot halves

1 cup dried pear halves

1 cup pitted prunes

1 cup dried peach halves

3 cups water

¼ cup granulated brown sugar

NUTRITIONAL FACTS (PER SERVING)
Calories: 206   Carbohydrates: 53.8 g   Cholesterol: 0 mg
Fat: 0.5 g   Fiber: 6.1 g   Protein: 2.2 g   Sodium: 10 mg

Sweet Cooked Grapes

Yield: *8 servings*

2 pounds seedless green and/or red grapes, washed and removed from stems

2 tablespoons granulated sugar

Enjoy these sweet grapes by themselves or spoon a few over slices of chilled cantaloupe or honeydew. They are also a delicious addition to your favorite breakfast cereal.

1. Place the grapes in a small saucepan with enough water to almost cover.

2. Cover the pan and cook over medium heat for 10 minutes. Reduce the heat to low and simmer for 10 minutes.

3. Remove from the heat and add the sugar. Mix thoroughly.

4. Refrigerate until chilled. Spoon into bowls and serve.

NUTRITIONAL FACTS (PER SERVING)
Calories: 81   Carbohydrates: 21.7 g   Cholesterol: 0 mg
Fat: 0.5 g   Fiber: 1.4 g   Protein: 0.7 g   Sodium: 2 mg

Cooked Strawberries

Yield: *8 servings*

2 quarts ripe strawberries, washed and hulled*

2 tablespoons granulated sugar

* Can use 12-ounce package frozen strawberries, thawed. If using frozen strawberries, reduce the cooking time to 5 minutes.

Spoon these luscious strawberries over fresh fruit salads or slices of melon. Or serve them in the center of a halved cantaloupe or honeydew.

1. Place the strawberries in a small saucepan with enough water to almost cover. Add the sugar and mix thoroughly.

2. Cover the pan and cook over medium heat for 10 minutes.

3. Refrigerate until chilled. Spoon into bowls and serve.

NUTRITIONAL FACTS (PER SERVING)
Calories: 54   Carbohydrates: 13 g   Cholesterol: 0 mg
Fat: 0.5 g   Fiber: 3.2 g   Protein: 0.9 g   Sodium: 1 mg

Ripe Peach Compote

The wonderful taste of ripe peaches makes this summer dessert a real winner.

1. Place all of the ingredients in a microwave-safe baking dish. Cover with wax paper and microwave for 5 minutes on High, or until the peaches are soft.

2. Refrigerate for 30 minutes.

3. Spoon into individual bowls and serve.

Yield: *8 servings*

2 pounds ripe peaches, washed, sliced, and pitted

1/4 cup sugar granulated brown sugar

3 cups water

NUTRITIONAL FACTS (PER SERVING)
Calories: 54   Carbohydrates: 14 g   Cholesterol: 0 mg
Fat: 0.1 g   Fiber: 1.7 g   Protein: 0.6 g   Sodium: 3 mg

VARIATIONS

• Use any of your favorite fruits or fruit combinations for this compote.

• You can also cook this compote in a covered saucepan over medium heat. Cooking time is about 15 minutes.

Creamy Rice Pudding

Yield: *12 servings*

1 cup brown rice

2 quarts skim milk

1 cup granulated brown sugar

1 medium egg white

1 tablespoon vanilla extract

¼ teaspoon ground cinnamon

Think it's impossible to create a low-fat rice pudding that is creamy and delicious? This recipe will change your mind.

1. Bring 2½ cups of water to a boil in a small saucepan. Stir in the rice, reduce the heat to low, and cover. Cook for 35 minutes, or until the rice is tender and easily fluffs with a fork.

2. Bring the milk and sugar to boil in a large saucepan. Stir in the rice and egg white, reduce the heat to low, and simmer 3 to 4 minutes. Add the vanilla.

3. Pour the mixture into a medium serving bowl, sprinkle with cinnamon, and refrigerate for 30 minutes.

4. Spoon the chilled rice pudding into individual serving bowls and enjoy.

NUTRITIONAL FACTS (PER SERVING)

Calories: 162   Carbohydrates: 31.9 g   Cholesterol: 3 mg
Fat: 0.7 g   Fiber: 0 g   Protein: 7.1 g   Sodium: 94 mg

VARIATION

- To reduce the cooking time, use instant rice instead of the longer-cooking variety.

Honeydew with Strawberry Sauce

Picture perfect every time.

Yield: *8 servings*

1. Place the strawberries, sugar, and lemon juice in a blender or food processor and purée for 10 seconds.

2. Place the honeydew in a serving bowl and top with the purée.

3. Serve immediately or place in the refrigerator until chilled.

4 cups fresh honeydew chunks*

4 cups fresh strawberries, washed and hulled*

¼ cup granulated sugar

1 tablespoon lemon juice

* Can use frozen variety that has been thawed.

NUTRITIONAL FACTS (PER SERVING)
Calories: 59   Carbohydrates: 14.9 g   Cholesterol: 0 mg
Fat: 0.3 g   Fiber: 1.9 g   Protein: 0.6 g   Sodium: 5 mg

VARIATION

• Try this sweet strawberry sauce over sorbet or fresh berries.

Alana's Creamy Pumpkin Muffins

Yield: *12 Muffins*

1 1/2 cups whole wheat flour

1/4 cup granulated brown sugar

1/2 teaspoon baking soda

1/4 teaspoon baking powder

1 teaspoon ground cinnamon

1/4 teaspoon ground ginger

2 tablespoons canned pumpkin

2 tablespoons unsweetened applesauce

2/3 cup frozen apple juice concentrate, thawed

1 medium egg white

Even nonpumpkin lovers will enjoy these luscious muffins.

1. Preheat the oven to 350°F. Lightly coat a muffin tin with cooking spray or line with paper muffin cups. Set aside.

2. Combine the flour, brown sugar, baking soda, baking powder, cinnamon, and ginger in a large bowl.

3. In another bowl, combine the pumpkin, applesauce, apple juice, and egg white. Pour into the flour mixture and stir until just mixed. Do not overstir.

4. Spoon the batter into the muffin tin. Fill each cup about ¾ full.

5. Bake for 20 minutes or until a toothpick inserted into the center of a muffin comes out clean.

6. Cool the muffins at least 10 minutes before removing from the tin. Serve warm, at room temperature, or chilled.

NUTRITIONAL FACTS (PER MUFFIN)
Calories: 92   Carbohydrates: 21 g   Cholesterol: 0 mg
Fat: 0.4 g   Fiber: 2.1 g   Protein: 2.5 g   Sodium: 71 mg

Alana's Zuperb Zucchini Muffins

These flavorful muffins are so sweet and moist, you'll find it hard to believe that they're made with zucchini.

1. Preheat the oven to 350°F. Lightly coat a muffin tin with cooking spray or line with paper muffin cups. Set aside.

2. Place the zucchini and apple juice in a blender or food processor and purée for 10 seconds.

3. Combine the flour, brown sugar, baking soda, baking powder, cinnamon, and nutmeg in a large bowl. Add the egg white and mix well. Stir in the zucchini purée until just mixed. Do not overstir.

4. Spoon the batter into the muffin tin. Fill each cup about ¾ full.

5. Bake for 20 minutes or until a toothpick inserted into the center of a muffin comes out clean.

6. Cool the muffins at least 10 minutes before removing from the tin. Serve warm, at room temperature, or chilled.

Yield: *12 Muffins*

1 cup frozen zucchini slices, thawed and drained

¹/₂ cup frozen apple juice concentrate, thawed

1¹/₂ cups whole wheat flour

¹/₄ cup granulated brown sugar

¹/₂ teaspoon baking soda

¹/₄ teaspoon baking powder

1 teaspoon ground cinnamon

¹/₂ teaspoon ground nutmeg

1 medium egg white

NUTRITIONAL FACTS (PER MUFFIN)

Calories: 86   Carbohydrates: 19.2 g   Cholesterol: 0 mg
Fat: 0.4 g   Fiber: 2.1 g   Protein: 2.4 g   Sodium: 70 mg

Fresh Cranberry Loaf

Yield: *8-x-4-inch loaf*

1 1/2 cups unbleached all-purpose flour

1 cup oat bran

1/4 cup granulated brown sugar

1/2 teaspoon baking soda

1/4 teaspoon baking powder

1/2 teaspoon ground cinnamon

1/8 teaspoon ground allspice

1/4 cup applesauce with cranberries

1/2 cup orange juice

2 medium egg whites

1 cup fresh cranberries

This cake has a wonderful tart taste and creamy texture.

1. Preheat the oven to 350°F. Coat an 8-x-4-inch loaf pan with cooking spray and set aside.

2. Combine the flour, oat bran, brown sugar, baking soda, baking powder, cinnamon, and allspice in a large bowl.

3. In another bowl, mix together the applesauce, orange juice, and egg whites. Pour this mixture into the flour mixture and stir until just mixed. Do not overstir. Gently fold in the cranberries.

4. Spoon the batter into the muffin tin. Fill each cup about 3/4 full.

5. Bake for 20 minutes or until a toothpick inserted into the center of the loaf comes out clean.

6. Allow to cool at least 10 minutes before slicing. Serve warm, at room temperature, or chilled.

NUTRITIONAL FACTS (PER SERVING)
Calories: 90   Carbohydrates: 20 g   Cholesterol: 0 mg
Fat: 0.7 g   Fiber: 1.5 g   Protein: 3.2 g   Sodium: 61 mg

Heavenly Blueberry-Oat Bran Muffins

These luscious blueberry muffins include the healthful benefits of oat bran.

Yield: *12 Muffins*

1 cup oat bran

1/2 cup unbleached all-purpose flour

1/4 cup granulated brown sugar

1/2 teaspoon baking soda

1/4 teaspoon baking powder

1/2 teaspoon ground cinnamon

4 tablespoons unsweetened applesauce

1/2 cup frozen apple juice concentrate, thawed

2 medium egg whites

1 cup fresh blueberries

1. Preheat the oven to 350°F. Lightly coat a muffin tin with cooking spray or line with paper muffin cups. Set aside.

2. Combine the oat bran, flour, brown sugar, baking soda, baking powder, and cinnamon in a large bowl.

3. In another bowl, combine the applesauce, apple juice, and egg whites. Pour into the flour mixture and stir until just mixed. Do not overstir. Gently fold in the blueberries.

4. Spoon the batter into the muffin tin. Fill each cup about 3/4 full.

5. Bake for 20 minutes or until a toothpick inserted into the center of a muffin comes out clean.

6. Cool the muffins at least 10 minutes before removing from the tin. Serve warm, at room temperature, or chilled.

NUTRITIONAL FACTS (PER MUFFIN)

Calories: 83   Carbohydrates: 19.9 g   Cholesterol: 0 mg
Fat: 0.8 g   Fiber: 1.8 g   Protein: 2.8 g   Sodium: 75 mg

VARIATION

• Adding 1/4 teaspoon of ground mace to the dry ingredients gives these muffins a unique flavor.

Meringue Puffs

Yield: *12 puffs*

2 medium egg whites

1 teaspoon vanilla extract

¼ cup granulated sugar

Whip up these delicious puffs whenever you need a quick and easy dessert.

1. Preheat the oven to 300°F. Coat a cookie sheet with cooking spray and set aside.

2. Using an electric mixer, beat the egg whites about 2 minutes or until they are stiff.

3. Add the vanilla and gradually beat in the sugar. Continue to beat until the mixture is stiff and satiny.

4. Drop teaspoons of the mixture onto the cookie sheet.

5. Bake for 20 minutes, or until the tops are light brown.

6. Allow the puffs to cool before removing from the cookie sheet.

NUTRITIONAL FACTS (PER PUFF)

Calories: 19   Carbohydrates: 4.3 g   Cholesterol: 0 mg

Fat: 0 g   Fiber: 0 g   Protein: 0.6 g   Sodium: 9 mg

VARIATIONS

- For chocolate-flavored puffs, use chocolate syrup instead of vanilla extract.
- Add ¼ cup of any of the following, in any combination: chopped walnuts, raisins, carob chips, chopped dried fruit.

Chewy Chocolate Chip Cookies

These cookies will melt in your mouth.

Yield: *40 cookies*

1. Preheat the oven to 375°F. Coat 2 large cookie sheets with cooking spray and set aside.

2. Combine the flour, baking powder, and baking soda in a medium bowl.

3. In another bowl, mix together the brown and granulated sugars. Add the prune butter and molasses, and mix well. Stir in the egg whites, vanilla, and water. Add the flour mixture, 1 cup at a time, stirring well after each addition. Gently fold in the chocolate chips.

4. Drop tablespoons of the batter onto the cookie sheets.

5. Bake for 9 to 10 minutes, or until the bottoms of the cookies are lightly browned.

6. Allow to cool before serving.

2¼ cups unbleached all-purpose flour

1 teaspoon baking powder

½ teaspoon baking soda

½ cup dark brown sugar, packed

½ cup granulated sugar

½ cup prune butter (lekvar)

1 tablespoon molasses

2 medium egg whites

1 tablespoon vanilla extract

1 tablespoon water

1 cup chocolate chips

NUTRITIONAL FACTS (PER COOKIE)

Calories: 69   Carbohydrates: 13.5 g   Cholesterol: 0 mg
Fat: 1.3 g   Fiber: 0.4 g   Protein: 1.1 g   Sodium: 28 mg

Grandma Helen's Hamantaschen

Yield: *25 pastries*

DOUGH

2 packages active dry yeast
($^1\!/4$ ounce each)

2 tablespoons warm water

2 cups unbleached all-purpose
flour

$^1\!/4$ cup pear baby food

1 cup granulated sugar

1 medium egg yolk

FILLING

6 tablespoons prune and/or
apricot butter

Hamantaschen are filled pastries that are traditionally eaten during the holiday of Purim. The egg yolk is necessary for a light, fluffy pastry dough.

1. Combine the yeast and warm water in a small bowl and let stand until foamy (about 5 minutes).* If the water does not foam, you can be sure the yeast is past its prime and will not cause the dough to rise. Discard it and begin again with fresh yeast.

2. In a small bowl, blend together the pears and $^1\!/4$ cup of the flour and set aside. Combine the remaining flour and sugar in a large bowl. Add the yeast and egg yolk, and blend well. Add the pear mixture and knead into a ball. Cover with plastic wrap and refrigerate for 8 hours or overnight.

3. Preheat the oven to 350°F. Coat 2 large cookie sheets with cooking spray and set aside.

4. On a floured board, roll out the chilled dough to $^1\!/4$-inch thickness. Using a 2-inch round cookie cutter (or the top of the same size water glass), cut out circles of dough. Place $^1\!/2$ teaspoon of prune and/or apricot butter on the center of each circle. Bring up the sides over the filling and press into a triangular shape. (*See* Forming Hamantaschen below.)

Forming Hamantaschen

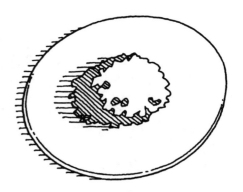

1. *Place the filling in the center of the circle.*

5. Place on cookie sheets and bake for 9 to 12 minutes, or until the hamantaschen are slightly brown on the bottom.

6. Allow to cool before serving.

* Be sure to use warm water only when checking (proofing) the yeast. If the water is too hot, it will kill the yeast. If the water is too cold, the yeast will work too slowly.

NUTRITIONAL FACTS (PER PASTRY)
Calories: 83   Carbohydrates: 18.2 g   Cholesterol: 9 mg
Fat: 0.3 g   Fiber: 0.3 g   Protein: 1.4 g   Sodium: 12 mg

VARIATIONS

• Feel free to use any fruit butter, jam, preserve, or jelly for the filling.

• Before baking the hamantaschen, brush the dough with beaten egg white.

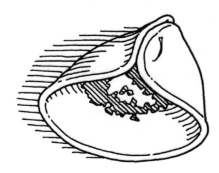

2. *Fold up the edges of the circle to form a triangular base.*

3. *Pinch the edges together, leaving a small opening in the center of the pastry.*

Easy-Bake Hamantaschen

Yield: *30 pastries*

These hamantaschen are so delicious you'll find it hard to believe that they're fat-free!

DOUGH

2¹/₂ cups unbleached
    all-purpose flour

1 teaspoon baking powder

1 cup granulated sugar

2 medium egg whites

¹/₄ cup pear baby food

1 tablespoon orange juice

1 tablespoon vanilla extract

FILLING

7 tablespoons prune and/or
    apricot butter

1. Combine the flour and baking powder in a large bowl and set aside.

2. In another bowl, combine the sugar, egg whites, pear baby food, orange juice, and vanilla. Stir into the flour mixture to form a dough. Shape the dough into a ball, cover with plastic wrap, and refrigerate for 1 hour.

3. When the dough is chilled, preheat the oven to 350°F. Coat 2 large cookie sheets with cooking spray and set aside.

4. On a floured board, roll out the chilled dough to ¹/₄-inch thickness. Using a 2-inch round cookie cutter (or the top of the same size water glass), cut out circles of dough. Place ¹/₂ teaspoon of prune or apricot butter on the center of each circle. Bring up the sides over the filling and press into a triangular shape. (*See* Forming Hamantaschen on page 205.)

5. Place on cookie sheets and bake for 9 to 12 minutes, or until the hamantaschen are slightly brown on the bottom.

6. Allow to cool before serving.

NUTRITIONAL FACTS (PER PASTRY)
Calories: 76   Carbohydrates: 16.9 g   Cholesterol: 0 mg
Fat: 0.1 g   Fiber: 0.2 g   Protein: 1.3 g   Sodium: 16 mg

VARIATIONS

• Feel free to use any fruit butter, jam, preserve, or jelly for the filling.

• Before baking the hamantaschen, brush the dough with beaten egg white.

Top Left: Easy-Bake Hamantaschen (page 206)
Right: Fresh Cranberry Loaf (page 200)
Center: Kiwi Parfait (page 193) and
Blueberry Parfait (page 192)

Top Left: Rosh Hashanah Honey Cake (page 207)

Center Right: Honeydew with Strawberry Sauce (page 197)

Bottom Right: Chewy Chocolate Chip Cookies (page 203)

Rosh Hashanah Honey Cake

Symbolizing the wish for a sweet new year, honey cake is a traditional dessert for Rosh Hashanah, the Jewish New Year.

1. Preheat the oven to 350°F. Coat a 9-inch springform pan with cooking spray and set aside.

2. Combine the flour, baking powder, baking soda, and cinnamon in a medium bowl.

3. In another bowl, mix the egg whites and prune butter until well-blended. Stir in the honey, apple juice, and coffee and mix well. Add the flour mixture, 1 cup at a time, stirring well after each addition. Fold in the apple and walnuts.

4. Pour the batter into the springform pan.

5. Bake for 55 minutes or until a toothpick inserted in the center of the cake comes out dry.

6. Let the cake cool for 10 to 15 minutes before removing from the pan. Serve at room temperature.

Yield: *9-inch round cake*

3$1/2$ cups unbleached all-purpose flour

1 tablespoon baking powder

1 teaspoon baking soda

1 teaspoon ground cinnamon

4 medium egg whites

2 tablespoons prune butter (lekvar)

$3/4$ cup honey

$1/4$ cup frozen apple juice concentrate, thawed

1 cup black coffee

1 tablespoon grated apple, or unsweetened applesauce

$1/4$ cup chopped walnuts.

NUTRITIONAL FACTS (PER SERVING)
Calories: 135   Carbohydrates: 29.9 g   Cholesterol: 0 mg
Fat: 0.4 g   Fiber: 0.2 g   Protein: 3.1 g   Sodium: 130 mg

VARIATION

- For a delicate taste of orange, add 1 teaspoon of grated orange rind to the batter.

Cheese Blintzes

Yield: *12 blintzes*

CRÊPE BATTER

1 1/4 cups unbleached
  all-purpose flour

3/4 cup skim milk

1/4 cup unsweetened
  applesauce

3 medium egg whites

1 tablespoon granulated brown
  sugar

1 teaspoon baking powder

FILLING

16 ounces fat-free cottage
  cheese

4 ounces fat-free cream cheese

2 medium egg whites

2 tablespoons granulated
  brown sugar

This traditional dairy dish for the holiday of Shavuous can be made with a variety of luscious fillings.

1. Stir the batter ingredients together in a medium bowl until smooth.

2. Coat an 8-inch nonstick skillet with cooking spray. Place over medium heat until the skillet is hot but not smoking.

3. Spoon about 1/3 cup of batter into the skillet and tilt the pan from side to side until the batter covers the bottom. Cook 2 minutes or until the bottom of the crêpe is golden brown. Remove and place on a paper towel. Repeat with the remaining batter.

4. Combine the filling ingredients in a large bowl and blend until smooth.

5. Place a crêpe, golden brown side up, on a plate. Spoon 2 tablespoons of filling in the center. Fold the right and left sides over the filling, then fold up the remaining sides so they overlap. (*See* Forming a Blintz below.) Repeat with the remaining crêpes and filling.

6. Coat the skillet with cooking spray and place over medium heat. Place 2 to 3 blintzes at a time in the skillet, seam side down. Cook for 2 minutes on each side.

7. Serve with fat-free sour cream or applesauce.

1. Place the filling in the center of the crêpe.

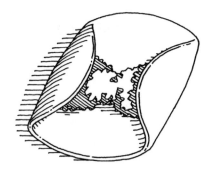

2. Fold the right and left sides over the filling.

Forming a Blintz

NUTRITIONAL FACTS (PER BLINTZ)
Calories: 119   Carbohydrates: 19.6 g   Cholesterol: 3 mg
Fat: 0.2 g   Fiber: 0.1 g   Protein: 8.8 g   Sodium: 252 mg

VARIATIONS

- Add 3 tablespoons of your favorite preserves to the filling. Blueberry, cherry, and strawberry are good choices.

- Try the cherry cheese filling used in Cherry Cheese Knishes (page 211).

- For potato blintzes, try the filling used in Potato Knishes (page 24).

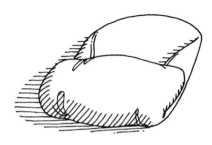

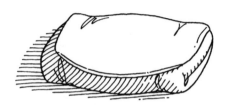

3. *Fold up the remaining sides so they overlap.*   **4.** *The completed blintz.*

Blintz Casserole

Yield: *12 servings*

A new twist on the traditional cheese blintz.

CRÊPE BATTER

1 1/4 cups unbleached
   all-purpose flour

1 teaspoon baking powder

1 tablespoon granulated brown
   sugar

3/4 cup skim milk

3 medium egg whites

1/4 cup unsweetened
   applesauce

FILLING

16 ounces fat-free cottage
   cheese

4 ounces fat-free cream cheese,
   softened

1 tablespoon fat-free sour cream

2 tablespoons granulated
   brown sugar

2 medium egg whites

3 tablespoons strawberry
   preserves

1. Preheat the oven to 350°F. Coat a 9-x-13 inch baking dish with cooking spray.

2. Using a spoon, blend the crêpe batter ingredients together in a large bowl until smooth. In another bowl, blend together the filling ingredients.

3. Spoon half the crêpe batter in an even layer on the bottom of the baking dish. Spoon the filling mixture over the batter. Top with the remaining batter.

4. Bake uncovered for 1 hour, or until the top is cooked and the edges are slightly browned.

5. Allow to sit for 10 minutes, before cutting into squares and serving with fat-free sour cream or applesauce.

NUTRITIONAL FACTS (PER SERVING)

Calories: 119   Carbohydrates: 19.6 g   Cholesterol: 3 mg
Fat: 0.2 g   Fiber: 0.1 g   Protein: 8.8 g   Sodium: 252 mg

Cherry Cheese Knishes

These knishes are a wonderful old-fashioned dessert treat.

Yield: *15 knishes*

1. Combine the yeast and warm water in a small bowl and let it stand until foamy (about 5 minutes).* If the water does not foam, you can be sure the yeast is past its prime and will not cause the dough to rise. Discard it and begin again with fresh yeast.

2. In a small bowl, blend together the pears and ¼ cup of the flour and set aside. Combine the remaining flour and sugar in a large bowl. Add the yeast and the unbeaten egg white, and blend well. Add the pear mixture and knead into a ball. Cover with plastic wrap and refrigerate 5 to 6 hours (may be refrigerated overnight).

3. Preheat the oven to 350°F. Coat 2 large cookie sheets with cooking spray and set aside. Combine the filling ingredients in a small bowl.

4. On a floured board, roll out the chilled dough to ¼-inch thickness. Using a sharp knife, cut the dough into 4-x-5-inch rectangles, and place 1 tablespoon of filling in the center of each. Fold the right and left sides over the filling, then fold up the remaining sides so they overlap. (*See* Forming a Knish on page 25.)

5. Place the knishes on the cookie sheets, brush with the beaten egg white, and bake for 20 to 25 minutes, or until lightly browned.

6. Allow to cool before serving.

* Be sure to use warm water only when checking (proofing) the yeast. If the water is too hot, it will kill the yeast. If the water is too cold, the yeast will work too slowly.

DOUGH

2 packages dry yeast (¼ ounce each)

2 tablespoons warm water

2 cups unbleached all-purpose flour

¼ cup pear baby food

1 cup granulated sugar

1 medium egg white, unbeaten

1 medium egg white, beaten

FILLING

4 ounces farmer cheese

2 tablespoons cherry preserves

NUTRITIONAL FACTS (PER KNISH)

Calories: 145   Carbohydrates: 28.7 g   Cholesterol: 4 mg
Fat: 1.3 g   Fiber: 0.4 g   Protein: 5 g   Sodium: 61 mg

Metric Conversion Tables

Common Liquid Conversions

Measurement	=	Milliliters
$1/4$ teaspoon	=	1.25 milliliters
$1/2$ teaspoon	=	2.50 milliliters
$3/4$ teaspoon	=	3.75 milliliters
1 teaspoon	=	5.00 milliliters
$1^{1}/4$ teaspoons	=	6.25 milliliters
$1^{1}/2$ teaspoons	=	7.50 milliliters
$1^{3}/4$ teaspoons	=	8.75 milliliters
2 teaspoons	=	10.0 milliliters
1 tablespoon	=	15.0 milliliters
2 tablespoons	=	30.0 milliliters

Measurement	=	Liters
$1/4$ cup	=	0.06 liters
$1/2$ cup	=	0.12 liters
$3/4$ cup	=	0.18 liters
1 cup	=	0.24 liters
$1^{1}/4$ cups	=	0.30 liters
$1^{1}/2$ cups	=	0.36 liters
2 cups	=	0.48 liters
$2^{1}/2$ cups	=	0.60 liters
3 cups	=	0.72 liters
$3^{1}/2$ cups	=	0.84 liters
4 cups	=	0.96 liters
$4^{1}/2$ cups	=	1.08 liters
5 cups	=	1.20 liters
$5^{1}/2$ cups	=	1.32 liters

Converting Fahrenheit to Celsius

Fahrenheit	=	Celsius
200—205	=	95
220—225	=	105
245—250	=	120
275	=	135
300—305	=	150
325—330	=	165
345—350	=	175
370—375	=	190
400—405	=	205
425—430	=	220
445—450	=	230
470—475	=	245
500	=	260

Conversion Formulas

LIQUID When You Know	Multiply By	To Determine
teaspoons	5.0	milliliters
tablespoons	15.0	milliliters
fluid ounces	30.0	milliliters
cups	0.24	liters
pints	0.47	liters
quarts	0.95	liters

WEIGHT When You Know	Multiply By	To Determine
ounces	28.0	grams
pounds	0.45	kilograms

Index